W9-ANK-768

LONELINESS:

ISSUES OF EMOTIONAL LIVING
IN AN AGE OF STRESS
FOR CLERGY AND RELIGIOUS

LONELINESS:

ISSUES OF EMOTIONAL LIVING
IN AN AGE OF STRESS
FOR CLERGY AND RELIGIOUS

THE SECOND BOSTON
PSYCHOTHEOLOGICAL SYMPOSIUM

ANNA POLCINO

JOSEPH L. HART

BERNARD J. BUSH

RICHARD GILMARTIN

Edited by James P. Madden

With a Foreword by Thomas A. Kane

AFFIRMATION BOOKS
WHITINSVILLE, MASSACHUSETTS

PUBLISHED WITH ECCLESIASTICAL PERMISSION

First Edition
© 1977 by House of Affirmation, Inc.

All rights reserved, including the right of reproduction in whole or in part, in any form or by any means, electronic or mechanical, including photocopying, recording, or by any information storage and retrieval system, without permission in writing from the publisher. Inquiries should be addressed to Affirmation Books, 456 Hill Street, Whitinsville, MA 01588.

Printed by Mercantile Printing Company, Worcester, MA
United States of America

To

present and former residents

of the House of Affirmation

with love and gratitude

248.4

M ea. L

CONTENTS

FOREWORD

Reading this book will dispel neither your loneliness nor mine, but it may help us to acknowledge and accept some of our feelings of loneliness. The essays herein represent an honest sharing of both personal reflections and clinical expertise.

The non-affirmed person displays a life style marked by "doing," by workaholism and escapism, always in an effort to run away from loneliness. The non-affirmed person looks to work, power, possessions, pleasing people, and "killing time" as ways of evading the reality of loneliness.

Several years ago Clark Moustakas wrote a book entitled *Loneliness* in which he distinguished two types of loneliness: loneliness anxiety and existential loneliness. Loneliness anxiety is what non-affirmed persons suffer. It is fundamentally a breach between what a person is and what he or she pretends to be. Lonely persons so dread their loneliness that they are engaged in a continual attempt to escape it. But their efforts are futile. No crowd, no title, no new "authentic psychological theory" can take away the reality that each of us is existentially a solitary individual, that each of us is *uniquely* alone in this world. Existential loneliness is our awareness of ourselves as solitary persons. Moustakas's book urges that we "let be" our loneliness. Our separateness offers us the opportunity to grow in awareness of creative loneliness, the experience of which gives us a sense of solitude and isolation whereby we learn about our relatedness to others and to all of creation.

The affirmed person does not run away from loneliness but experiences it as an existential reality. The affirmed

9

person shares his or her being lonely and in sharing it comes to a new knowledge and feeling of self. Moustakas speaks of this experience when he writes:

> We must care for our own loneliness and suffering and the loneliness and suffering of others, for within pain and isolation and loneliness one can find courage and hope and what is brave and lovely and true in life. Seeing loneliness is a way to self-identity and to love, and faith in the wonder of living. . . . Loneliness leaves its traces in man but these are marks of pathos, of weathering, which enhance dignity and maturity and beauty, and which open new possibilities for tenderness and love. . . . Loneliness is as much a reality of life as night and rain and thunder and it can be lived creatively. So I say let there be loneliness, for where there is loneliness, there is also sensitivity, there is awareness and recognition of promise. [p. 103]

It is with pride that I recommend the following essays by my colleagues. These essays will help you reflect on your own natural situation of being alone and help you relate to this fundamental wound that exists in the heart and soul of each of us.

I am most appreciative to Father James J. Madden, C.S.C., the editor of this book, and to Sister Mary Dennis Donovan, C.S.J., for assisting him. Moreover, I am especially grateful to those persons who allow us members of the psychotheological therapeutic community to participate with them in their struggles in times of stress, anxiety, and loneliness. These relationships have developed into continuing friendships of great meaning.

Thomas A. Kane, Ph.D., D.P.S.
Priest, Diocese of Worcester
International Executive Director
House of Affirmation, Inc.

PREFACE

The five essays in this volume are the fruit of a one-day symposium sponsored by the House of Affirmation, International Therapeutic Center for Clergy and Religious, and held at Aquinas Junior College, Newton, Massachusetts, on October 2, 1976. A follow-up to last year's symposium on the topic of coping, this symposium had as its topic loneliness, a theme chosen because it was requested by so many individuals who attended the symposium last year.

Thus the words of this book were spoken before they were printed. Albeit the printed word often loses the zest and spirit of the spoken word, the original lectures have not been rewritten but appear in the informal style in which they were first spoken. They retain the informative yet relaxed flavor of the day's events. Unfortunately, the drama performed by Sister Eileen Horan, R.S.M., which expressed the theme of loneliness to holiness so humanly and poignantly, cannot be conveyed fully in the written word. Her performance expressed in a profound way the healing touch of affirmation.

Loneliness is part of the human condition. Since to be human is to be lonely, there are no simple solutions to the problem of loneliness. Distractions can diminish the pain of loneliness, but ultimately they will fail to meet the problem at its deepest level. Attempting to ignore loneliness will only intensify its effects, for there is no escape from this condition that touches the inner core of a person's being.

Loneliness can be humanity's greatest dignity or its heaviest burden. It can be creative or destructive. Obviously, it is not joyful; on the contrary, its pain is often unbearable. To pretend otherwise is foolish and solves nothing. Yet when we actually confront loneliness, or rather, our fear of it, we realize that our attitude toward loneliness and not the condition itself creates the problem. So why not try to discover the positive side of loneliness? Why not seek its value? Why allow ourselves to succumb to its destructive nature and thus to intensify its pain?

At the center of every one of us is an impenetrable and incommunicable area of longing that cannot be answered by the person alone. Our desires and yearnings for life, knowledge, joy, and peace far surpass our human limitations and ultimately can be satisfied by the unlimited God alone. Even the close relationship of a happily married couple cannot solve the problem of humanity's yearnings. No two persons can totally and completely communicate with each other despite their closeness and mutual understanding because at his or her impenetrable core each person is unique. Human closeness has its place, and deep human friendships answer many longings, but some loneliness will always remain as a testament to our individuality and uniqueness. Only God who understands and fathoms this uniqueness can respond to it.

No one individual, nor any one community, can adequately answer a person's needs. The loneliness of a celibate is not unique to him or her, or to other celibates. Loneliness is a universally human experience which should impel us to a more vital relationship with the living God, who exerts his call through felt loneliness. By impelling us to seek and respond to God, loneliness can be a growth value. We humans must support one another in the loneliness we experience. Part of that support must focus on warmth, understanding, and affirmation; another part must focus on mutual encouragement of a greater response to God in our lives.

The symposium addressed loneliness in the lives of religious professionals today. The essays vary considerably. The first essay is a commentary on the labyrinthine pathway the soul travels on its journey from loneliness to holiness, as personified in a drama of therapy. A second essay discusses the perils of the "pleaser" who suffers loneliness as well as other intrapersonal and interpersonal problems as a result of his or her failure to communicate truthfully with self and others. The third essay examines the conflicting loyalties of religious and clergy who remain enmeshed with family and whose loneliness and guilt are disguised as charity. A fourth essay differentiates healthy existential loneliness and unhealthy narcissism, a type of loneliness that comes about as a reaction to frustrated identity. The last essay, "Healing Grace," was not presented at the symposium and was first published in *The Way*, a British periodical. With the kind permission of the editor, James Walsh, S.J., "Healing Grace" has been reprinted in this volume both because it speaks insightfully about loneliness and because it incorporates a brief history of the House of Affirmation, its philosophy, and its purpose.

We at the House of Affirmation have seen how destructive and counterproductive loneliness can be. We have witnessed much maladaptive and unsuccessful integration in some lives. Our hope is that by efforts such as this symposium we shall be instrumental in spreading the word of health and healing through authentic affirmation of persons.

A word of sincere gratitude is in order to all who have

made this year's symposium successful beyond our expectations. I would like to thank the program participants for sharing themselves and their expertise and the House of Affirmation staff, residents, and former residents who circulated to spread the good news about our ministry. I am especially grateful to the Sisters of St. Joseph for their generosity in making available to us for the second time their facilities at Aquinas Junior College and for remaining on hand to help when needed. Finally, I wish to thank the many individuals who attended the October symposium. Their willingness to brave the damp and rainy elements spoke eloquently to all of us who organized the program.

James P. Madden, C.S.C.
Boston, Massachusetts
March 1, 1977

Sister Anna Polcino, S.C.M.M., M.D., is founder and psychiatric director of the House of Affirmation, International Therapeutic Center for Clergy and Religious, Whitinsville, Massachusetts, and instructor in psychiatry at the University of Massachusetts Medical School, Worcester. A member of the Medical Mission Sisters since 1949, Sister Doctor Polcino received her medical degree from the Woman's Medical College of Pennsylvania. Following a surgical residency at Hahnemann Hospital, Philadelphia, she worked for nine years as a missionary surgeon and medical director at Holy Family Hospital, Karachi, West Pakistan, and Dacca, Bangladesh. She then returned to the United States and completed a psychiatric residency at Worcester State Hospital. She is founder and former psychiatric director of the Mental Health Clinic of the Green Island Neighborhood Opportunity Center in Worcester and of the Valley Adult Counseling Service in Linwood, Massachusetts. She is also founder and psychiatric director of the Worcester Diocese Consulting Center for Clergy and Religious. A member of the American Psychiatric Association, the American Medical Association, the Massachusetts Medical Society, and the National Federation of Catholic Physicians, Sister Doctor Polcino is current president of the National Guild of Catholic Psychiatrists. Acknowledged internationally for her work in psychiatry, she has been psychotherapist, lecturer, and psychiatric consultant to religious congregations in North America, Europe, and Asia.

FROM LONELINESS TO HOLINESS

Anna Polcino
with
Eileen Horan

The existential experience of loneliness can lead us to a solitude of soul whereby we become whole and holy, whereby we learn what it means to "be still and know that I am God" (Psalms 46:10). While experiencing existential loneliness, we ceaselessly question ourselves, others, our world, and even our God, demanding significant answers that make a lasting impact on our lives. Our questioning offers us the opportunity to discover and then know ourselves, our relation to others and to God, and our place in our world. Through an apparent breakdown of meaning, we find real meaning. We realize that by learning to be alone with ourselves we learn to be with and for others, that in the solitude of soul found in loneliness we discover the threads that bind the human community, and that by first moving away from others we encounter our real selves and God and are then able to move more genuinely toward others.

When many months ago I was asked to speak at this symposium, I intended to write a treatise wherein I would develop the thesis expressed above. For weeks my mind was filled with ideas for this treatise and with worries about its completion. Books and notes began to cover my desk; wads of crumpled and discarded papers became scattered about my office. I began to feel crowded, as if there were no room for me. I began feeling lonely. Then last night, I attended the performance of a drama that ex-

17

pressed all I had to say about loneliness to holiness with more clarity, immediacy, and eloquence than I could ever hope to convey. Having for weeks been crowded into an intellectual corner, smothered by abstract words and ideas, frustrated by my inability to breathe life into these abstractions even while polishing my text, I suddenly was experiencing—seeing, hearing, feeling—my thesis. The performance was the intellectual expression of my ideas given a physical and spiritual dimension. Actually moved to tears, I knew that those attending the symposium should share this lived experience. I knew that this performance, not my text, was the essence of our experience of loneliness to holiness.

When last night Sister Eileen Horan, R.S.M., first performed her interpretive dance and monologue, she had no idea she would be performing it again today at the symposium. For the last two years, we at the House of Affirmation have wanted to invite all former residents of the House to return for a weekend. Because this year the third anniversary of the founding of the House on the Feast of Saint Theresa, October 1, 1973, coincides with my Silver Jubilee on October 3, we decided to extend the invitation to our former residents for this weekend and to schedule the symposium today, October 2. We have always scheduled the symposium in conjunction with the founding, but this year we hoped that all former residents would attend the symposium and join with our current residents to help us celebrate both the founding of the House and my twenty-five years of religious profession. Sister Eileen's performance last night at the House was in honor of this celebration.

Sister Eileen knows the House well. She was a resident there for many months about two years ago, and I was her therapist. A Sister of Mercy of Rhode Island, she received her master's degree in drama from Emerson College, Boston.

Her dramatic talents are many, to which her performance will attest. But more importantly, Sister Eileen's performance attests to her having traveled the road from loneliness to holiness. In psychotherapy, Sister Eileen encountered her loneliness and let it lead her (admittedly only after much struggle) to that solitude of soul whereby we become whole and holy. She has thanked me (her drama is entitled *Gratiae Tante, Anna*) for having helped her along the way, for having given her new life and new hope. I was able to help because I too have encountered loneliness. I too have explored the depths of solitude and emerged more whole and holy. By listening to the language of loneliness, I became sensitive to myself and to others. Obviously, Sister Eileen has become similarly sensitive. Alone with my treatise, my approach to it exacerbated my loneliness. Sister Eileen's drama was a reminder. Just as in therapy my acceptance, understanding, and concern had given her the courage to confront her loneliness, so her drama gave me the opportunity to recover myself. Sister Eileen's dramatic path from loneliness to holiness is my path and your path and the path of all human beings who finally approach their loneliness creatively.

Yet I do not mean to imply that the road from loneliness to holiness is ever easy; Sister Eileen's path was labyrinthine, beset with not only loneliness but depression, anxiety, guilt, frustration, anger, and much psychic anguish, more than many of us can imagine, and much more than most of us will ever experience. When Sister Eileen began therapy, she was silent for more than three months. Yet I knew intuitively what she was experiencing. She communicated with me through her silence. I patiently waited for her to speak. As her therapy progressed, she revealed to me the depths of her soul. Her soul spoke to my soul. Now as you watch and listen to her drama, her soul will speak to your soul as well. Sister Eileen will tell you what it means to experience existential loneliness, and you will know why I could not resist asking her to share with you what she has shared with me. Sister Eileen's very presence here, her public performance, attests to the great distance she has traveled on her road from loneliness to holiness since her months of silence two years ago. She wrote most of the words, developed the choreography, and chose the music for her drama. She is assisted by Reverend John Fitzgerald, another former resident of the House who has served as her technical advisor.

[The script of Sister Eileen's drama follows, punctuated by short commentaries by Sister Anna Polcino, M.D.]

GRATIAE TANTE, ANNA

A drama created in honor of and to thank Sister Anna Polcino, M.D., and dedicated to her, to all the former and present residents and staff, both clinical and non-clinical, of the House of Affirmation, and to the members of my own community, the Sisters of Mercy of Rhode Island, for their love, their support, and their concern as I have searched and as I continue to search today for God's will in my life.

I. Who Controls Me?
Music: "A Fifth of Beethoven"
Walter Murphy and the Big Apple Band

Although Sister Eileen remained silent during much of her early therapy, I knew she was questioning her own identity. In the depths of loneliness we each ask the question: who am I? In this section of her drama, Sister Eileen conveys the destructive effect of incessant change on our lives and of our resultant tendency to assume many identities, none of which is our own. Each time we have established a rhythm, a beat, by which we can cope with and adapt ourselves to one stimulus, we are confronted by another. Each time we think we know who we are, we are asked to be someone else. Eventually, unable to adapt to ever-increasing changes in the "beat" of our lives, we lose control. No longer sure of even our identity, we have no foundation upon which to build change, no pivot upon which to revolve. We are no longer able to integrate the stimuli that barrage us from every direction. In our attempts to be everyone, we are no one. Sister Eileen asks: "Who's in control?" She knows she is not, and she wonders if she can trust anyone to be so. Can she trust her therapist? She fears trust as much as she fears change; she fears loss of control of her own impulses; she feels threatened. Finally, although still unsure, still anxious, she reaches out to her therapist, admitting her loss of identity, her loss of control, and her willingness to trust her therapist to help her find herself. The therapist becomes a significant other who helps her admit and affirm both what she is and what she is experiencing.

Who controls me?
Who controls my being me?
Who controls me?
Who controls my being me?[1]
Who am I?

---

1. In this section and the one that follows, I am indebted to Reverend Thomas A. Kane for the ideas expressed in his books entitled *Who Controls Me?* (Hicksville, N. Y.: Exposition Press, 1974) and *The Healing Touch of Affirmation* (Whitinsville, Mass.: Affirmation Books, 1976).

Who are you?
Who are we?
Who are they?
Who am I?
Who are you?
Who are we?
Who are they?
Who's in control? Who's in control?
Control?
NO!
There's only change, further change, more change
Update
Innovate
Renovate
Amalgamate
Disintegrate
Reinstate
Limitate
Accommodate
Re-order
Re-structure
Start   again
Where's the direction? Where's my place?
Only change, further change, more change.
Control?
Who's in control?
It's not I.
Hey, I'll play the part, o-o-o-oh, Ye-h-h-h
Tell me of the mask to wear.
Move with the image, baby.
This is the way you see me.
Maybe that's what I am.
Check the way I move, babe.
Check the way I stand.
I'll play your image to the hilt
If that's what you want to see.
I can be most anything, just give me to the count of three.
Stay with the rhythm, move with the beat.
Mesmerized, hypnotized
Stay with the rhythm, move with the beat.
Mesmerized, hypnotized
This is the way I cope, friend, this is the way I cope.

Stay with the rhythm, move with the beat.
Then I control reality.
Change, change, no, don't change.
Change, change, no, don't change the beat.
Change, change, no, don't change.
Change, change, no, don't change the beat.
Don't threaten me.
Who changed the rhythm?
Who changed the beat?
Where's the set identity?
Who changed the rhythm?
Who changed the beat?
Where's the set identity?
Exploration, no.
Encounter, no.
Search, no.
Adventure, no.
Choose, no.
Respond, I can't.
Why the change?
Who's in control?
I've lost control.
Let me just move with the beat, man.
Let me just move with the beat.
Uncertainty
Insecurity
Lost ability
No identity
Choose fantasy
Deny reality
Oh, the change, further change, more change
Who's in control?
I've lost control.
Help me.
Hold me.
Heal me.
Yess-ss-ss-ss-sss
Liberate me.

II.   That's Life?   No music

     Disjunct thought, nursery rhymes, and machine-like
repetition characterize this section wherein Sister Eileen

conveys what modern technology does to our creative approach to life. She questions whether life has meaning if in order to survive we must become dehumanized automatons that respond to any and every stimulus, including inane appeals to purchase products advertised on television. Her therapy has given her hope "of being fully alive," creatively and humanly alive, but the "powerful beat" of "incessant change" and "constant yet subtle oppression of the mind's creative adaptation to life" make her wonder whether to "fit in" she must despair of ever knowing and controlling her own self. Her therapist has told her that she must risk in order to know. But she fears coming into contact with her own aggression, hostility, ambivalence, or general "incompleteness" with its attendant human shortcomings. Shouldn't she take the "safer path" and repeat the beat? Yet still hopeful, she embraces the "new way of thinking" called assertion.

Liberate me.
Help me.
Hold me.
Heal me.

Liberate me from the bonds of my own slavery,
  from the chains of my own thought,
  from the shackles I've learned were not of my making.

I want to do certain things,
  be certain things,
  say certain things,
  love certain people and be loved by them.

I want to believe that I have a unique contribution to make to this world and that I cannot be truly myself unless I am able to make it. Unless I can truly love for all I'm worth, then I shall not care to be alive.

Alive?
Me?
Full of life?
Oh-h-h-h

Just the image of being fully alive; it makes me want to hope,
Really hope.
But, sometimes, I look out there, way out there,
And I say,
That's life? Life?

On the one hand, incessant change demanding an ongoing, never-
ending adjustment. And on the other, a constant yet subtle
oppression of the mind's creative adaptation to life by means
of a battery of artificial standards and goals.

Life.
That's life?
Life?
For the rhythm of life has a powerful beat.
For the rhythm of life has a powerful beat.
For the rhythm of life has a powerful beat.
Repeat, repeat, repeat, repeat.
Repeat, repeat, repeat, repeat.
"Kelloggs, because your best days start with breakfast."
"Bayer, for the kind of relief you can't get from an aspirin substi-
tute."
"A & P, if we can't do it, nobody can."
"NBC sends you all the best."
Repeat, repeat, repeat, repeat.
Repeat, repeat, repeat, repeat.
Step the step, play the role.
Step the step, play the role.
All I have to do is fit in, right?
All I have to do is fit in.
Just a cog in the wheel
Just a cog in the wheel
Technology, Mass-s-s-s production
Technology, Mass-s-s-s production
All I have to do is fit in, right?
All I have to do is fit in.
One, two, buckle ma shoe.
Three, four, shut de door.
Five, six, pick up sticks.
Seven, eight, lay 'dem straight.
Repeat, repeat, repeat, repeat.
All I have to do is fit in, right?
All I have to do is fit in.
Mary had a little lamb.

It's fle-e-ece was whi-i-ite as sno-o-ow.
And everywhere that Mary went,
That damn lamb was sure to go.
All I have to do is fit in, right?
All I have to do is fit in.
Pease porridge hot, pease porridge cold,
Pease porridge in the pot nine days old.
All I have to do is fit in, right?
All I have to do is fit in.
Mistress Mary, quite contrary,
How does your garden grow?
With silver bells and cockleshells
And pretty maids all in a row.
All in a row
All in a row
All in a row
All in a row
Repeat, repeat, repeat, repeat.
Technology, mass-s-s production
Technology, mass-s-s production
Tell me what to eat.
Tell me what to wear.
Tell me where to go.
And tell me how to get there.
Tell me what to eat.
Tell me what to wear.
Tell me where to go.
And tell me how to get there.
All I have to do is fit in, right?
Do I really want a place in the history of man?
Have we ever truly gained a new understanding of ourselves?
So much oppression
Both obvious and subtle
And so much revolution
I too revolt.
I struggle to be free.
Oh, not to subdue again,
Not to oppress another in any form,
But only to change, to grow,
To learn to live with my own incompleteness
And to let that incompleteness
Help me become one with the created order of the entire universe,

And thus move toward identity.
Oh, God, I hate to repeat, repeat.
But I fear working with that which is incomplete.
'tis almost better,
'tis so much safer to
Repeat, repeat, repeat, repeat
The safe path, the safe path.
Risk? Risk?
You want me to risk?
Revolve toward that which is most natural in all of us?
Recover my relationship with the world and with my god?
Risk, huh?
Risk, r . . . i . . . s . . . k
"Throw it off.
Cast it aside.
Put on the new man."[2]
Put on the new man.
Put on the new man.
Yeh?
Yeh Yeh-h-h. Y-E-H-H-H-H!
There's a new way of thinking.
There's a new way of thinking.
There's a new way of thinking.
It's gonna put me in motion.
There's a new way of thinking.
There's a new way of thinking.
There's a new way of thinking.
And it's called AS-SERTION!

III. Capisce?   Music: "Boogie-Woogie"
                                  Roper Dance Orchestra
                                  Roper Records

Therapy has taught Sister Eileen not to "play it safe,"
not to deny but to affirm and appreciate herself and her experiences. Significant others, her therapist and the members of the staff and residential community at the House
of Affirmation, have allowed her to be, to evolve, to work

---

2. Eph. 4:22-24. All biblical quotations are taken from *The
Jerusalem Bible* (New York: Doubleday, 1966).

herself out; they have offered her acceptance and support. But in this section, Sister Eileen reveals her continuing fear. She has begun to discover what she is and wants rather than what society wants her to be, but her discovery has made her feel angry, embarrassed, and foolish. She begs to retreat. Her new-found assertion waxes and wanes. She asks herself, as her therapist has asked: "capisce" (do you understand)? She has begun to understand, and here she concludes "assertion's the name of the game." But is the "game" any different from the "powerful beat"? Sister Eileen ponders this question in the next section and shares her great discovery with us.

ASSERT

Grab on to learning the most direct
For greater expression of affect.
Experiment and try new roles.
Don't play it safe with your head in a hole.
Don't rationalize,
And don't deny,
And never project,
But always reply.
O-o-o-o-o-oh, yeh.
Assert, assert
Assert, assert
Assert, assert
Oh, retreat, retreat
Please let me retreat.
Oh, let me retreat.
Express myself and be most firm.
Sometimes I think I'll never learn
Assertion's the name of this game.
Others are worth far more than I;
Their right to say no is greater than mine.
I've heard nice people never say no.
And since I'm a doll, how could it be so?
Redeem me from the incessant yes
And move me toward the salvific no.
O-o-o-o-o-oh, yeh!

Don't bother me, I can't cope.
Assertion's now my only hope.
I'll not back down.
You're out of line.
I'll go where you want,
Oh, no I won't.
This dress is too tight,
And it's rather short.
Don't bother to flirt;
It just doesn't work.
I'd like a raise
For the work I do.
Don't get the idea
I can't handle you.
No, I don't want any brooms today.
Oh, help my efforts to turn them away.
O-o-o-o-o-oh, yeh!
Oh, assertion
Dear assertion
Bless assertion
Yeh, assertion
Oh, assertion
Dear assertion
Bless assertion
Yeh, assertion
Prepare my script;
Write down my lines;
Observe my cues;
Hit them on time.
Oh, yes, I do have feelings today;
The things you drop are in my way;
Hold it on the salt if you please;
Hand me the pepper, I'd rather sneeze.
Bless my attempts at mastery.
Remove from me all futility.
I'm not Bo-Peep;
I've lost no sheep.
I'll not pretend to tolerate.
There's nothing now I'll mitigate.
Grab on to learning the most direct
For greater expression of affect.
Experiment and try new roles.

Don't play it safe with your head in a hole.
Don't rationalize,
And don't deny,
And never project,
But always reply.
O-o-o-o-oh, yeh!
Assert, assert
Assert, assert
Assert, assert
Capisce, capisce
Assert, assert
Capisce, capisce
Express myself and be most firm.
Sometimes I think I'll never learn.
Assertion's the name of the game.
Yeah!

IV.   Beneath the Surface   No music

The "game" and the "powerful beat" are surface reality, necessary to life, but not its essential meaning, which is found beneath the surface, "down deep, where you hurt and where I hurt, and where we both rejoice," where "it's not a game at all." At life's core abides the deeper, more meaningful reality, whose truth can speak to us only when we are still, only in silence. Here "immersed," we experience that solitude of soul whereby we become whole and holy. But Sister Eileen's discovery of this truth is fleeting. She cannot sustain her solitude as others have done whose solitude "clothes their nakedness with love." Her brief encounter with solitude leads again to loneliness—"no one" —which "strips [her] with the anguish of self-doubt and the absolute death of self-hate." But she persists; she plunges to the depths again, knowing she must "live," "feel," and "be torn by" her "intolerable loneliness" in order to emerge from it with a solitude of soul whereby "there shall be one." Yet repeatedly, at life's core, "as it was in the beginning," she finds only the unhealthy silence of her early days of therapy. She is unable to restore her glimpse of the stillness of solitude that speaks of the Word. She encounters "the rub" of loneliness, but she never loses hope of again being still and knowing God.

The game
Oh, yeh!
The game, the great big game
Only down deep,
Way down deep,
Where you hurt and where I hurt,
And where we both rejoice,
It's not a game at all.
It's life.
It's life,
And it says yes,
And it says no,
And it says come,
And it says let go.
But most of all,
Most of all,
It says be still,
       be still.
"Teach us to care and not to care,
And teach us to sit still."[3]
For if we do not understand your silence,
We shall never understand your words.
For the rhythm of life has a powerful beat.
For the rhythm of life has a powerful beat.
For the rhythm of life has a powerful beat.
Be still!
Be still!
Immersion in the stillness is immersion in the mystery
Is immersion in the Word, and the Word is Truth?
Be still!
Be still.
Oh,
But when I'm still,
When I am fully and totally alone,

---

3. T. S. Eliot, "Ash Wednesday," *Selected Poems* (New York: Harcourt, Brace and World, 1964).

Immersed in solitude,
Then so often
There is the deepest collision
"between my tormenting and my tormented self."[4]
God, "I'm up to Heaven and down to Hell in an hour."[5]
For others,
Their solitude clothes their nakedness with love.
But mine, mine strips me with the anguish of self-doubt and the
    absolute death of self-hate.
Stillness?
Emptiness.
Loneliness!
No . . . One
No one!
No one.
No-o-o-o
No-o-o-o.
Live with the no one.
Feel the no one.
Be torn by the no one,
And there shall be one.
There shall be one?
"The voice of love makes an emptiness and a solitude reverberate."[6]
The voice of love?
There shall be one?
"I will lead her into the wilderness and I will speak to her heart."[7]
There is only wilderness.
There is no word!
There shall be one?
In this intolerable loneliness, there shall be one?
As it was in the beginning?
Oh, there's the rub.
There's the rub.
As it was in the beginning . . .

V.   The Ultimate Prayer   Music: Prelude in C sharp minor
                                                  Rachmaninoff
                                                  Van Cliburn

---

4. May Sarton, *Journal of a Solitude* (New York: Norton, 1973).
5. Ibid.
6. François Mauriac, *Journal d'un homme de 30 ans*, as quoted in Sarton.
7. Hos. 2:16.

In loneliness our experience of time and space changes. We begin to look back at the past and relate the present and future to the past. Sister Eileen's hope of hearing the Word "as it was in the beginning" has caused her to ponder not only the beginning of her therapy, but the beginning of her life, from birth onward. She is aware of never having been touched by love, never having had her being affirmed by a significant other. She has been denied to such an extent that she has had "to pretend," "to choose . . . one thousand masks" in order to secure an identity. She admits: "I think I am,/But I am not." Unloved, unaffirmed, she has been "deeply wounded," suffering "great fear," "enormous guilt," "tormenting anxiety," and "much anticipation of total rejection." Life has been a series of "games," of "powerful beats" that she now describes as "ever-spinning, whirling circles" that push, pull, and pressure her to accommodate and assimilate change at a pace that is different from her own. Growing outwardly into an adult, a religious woman, she has remained inwardly a child, her growth stunted by the absence of love and the acceptance integral to it. Uncomprehending, she runs from herself, fearing the reality within her and fearing even more that there may be no reality. She yearns for the healing touch of affirmation, the "hand" of the "healer" for whom she will wait and to whom she will give her trust.

> "Every first thing continues forever with the child: the first color, the first music, the first flower paint the foreground of his life. The first inner and outer object of love, injustice, or such like throws a shadow immeasurably far along his after years."[8]

And so it begins.

---

8. Source unavailable.

My life begins.
At least I think it's life.
And I move,
And I perform,
And I reach out,
And I do all that I hope will allow love to touch me.
But it touches me not,
Not fully, not deeply.
And I think I am,
But I am not.
So full of empty spaces,
Of stark desert places.
For "what I say, I don't feel.
And what I feel, I don't show.
And what I show isn't real.
What is real, Lord, I don't know."[9]
And so I remain small
And deeply wounded
And terribly angry but know it not.
And so I learn to pretend
And to choose the one thousand masks that will secure me.
But with great fear
And enormous guilt
And tormenting anxiety
And so much anticipation of total rejection.
Yes, the desperate, pretending games
That hold the captive, trembling child within.
So much so
That all I know are circles,
Ever-spinning, whirling circles --
Up again around and down again around
And pulling and pushing and pressure, unbearable pressure.
To run, run
Don't stand still,
Don't look back,
For then you may know it as it really is.
And so I ran;
And so pretended,
In no way comprehending the Hell in my own life,
Forced to grow outwardly "with no voice for the infant cries and
        rages."[10]

---

9. Leonard Bernstein, *The Mass*, Columbia Records.
10. Sarton.

Yearning, burning to be touched
By a single, gentle hand.
"I need a way of seeing in the dark.
What way is this, what dark is this?"[11]
I need.
I need.
Is there no one?
"Whoever welcomes a child such as this welcomes me."[12]
No one?
"Free my soul from death,
 my eyes from tears,
 and my feet from stumbling."[13]
Say to me: Ephphatha, be opened.
Am I not worthy of the touching?
Put your fingers into my ears
And, spitting, touch my tongue.
Say to me:
Ephphatha, be opened
Ephphatha, be opened.[14]
Is there no hand?
Just one, to be His hand?
Is there no healer
To be His healer?
"And help me walk into the presence of the Lord, into the land of
 the living."[15]
No hand?
No healer?
"For you I wait all the day
And to you I give my trust unto safekeeping."[16]
VI. Her Name Was Anna

The therapist heals by affirming, by creating within her client a trust, an approval, an appreciation, and a reverence for who she is and who she can become. The therapist listens to her client's loneliness. Plummeting its inner depths together, the therapist and client emerge

11. Peter Shaffer, *Equus* (New York: Avon Books, 1974).

12. Mark 9:37.

13. Ps. 116.

14. Mark 7:33-34.

15. Ps. 16.

16. Ps. 25.

sharing that solitude of soul wherein all meaning lies. The therapist-healer serves as a guide, pointing the way to the ultimate Healer, to all that is and ever shall be. The therapist is ever a symbol of hope and renewal, a promise of psychological rebirth through the healing touch of affirmation, through the power of love. Affirmed herself, the therapist is able to be for others, never clinging, never possessing, always assisting the birth, careful to "clothe the child in love and trust/And then give it over to the calling of life itself when it is life's time."

Introduction   No music

And so I waited,
As we all have waited,
Knowing that we must have love
Even if there is no more of it in this world,
Knowing that the solitary agony of Christ
Is the agony of us all at certain moments.
Waiting,
Waiting for the one
Whose hand would be that of the Healer.
                     Music: "Nadia's Theme"
                              Perry Botkin, Jr.
                              from "Bless the Beasts and the Children"
And then the Father sent her.
Her name was Anna.
And to her I gave my trust
And laid bare the depths of my soul.
For you, Anna, are one
Whose hope is strong.
"You see and cherish all signs of life
And are truly ready at every moment
to help the birth of that which is ready to be born."[17]
Everyone of us here
And so many who are distant
Have been nourished by the immensity of your love
And the humaneness of your being.

---

17. Erich Fromm, *The Art of Loving* (New York: Harper and Row, 1956).

"In you, hope never ceases to surge up
And explore its own heights,
And your love,
Your love moves in a stillness to contemplate its own depths."[18]
You perform the most graceful healing, for you leave yourself
So exposed and vulnerable,
Letting the sore and wounded places within you
Reach out to tenderly touch another.[19]
Your beauty,
The radiance of the truth within you,
Never clings,
Never possesses.
You assist the birth,
Clothe the child in love and trust,
And then give it over to the calling of life itself when it is life's
     time.
And so we all pray to the Father in Heaven,
That He will bestow on you
Gifts in keeping with the riches of His glory.
May He strengthen you inwardly
Through the power of His Spirit.
May Christ always dwell in your heart through faith.
May love always be the root and foundation of your life.
And, Anna, may you experience always the fullness of God Him-
     self.[20]

I believe that after many years of suffering, Sister Eileen has received the fullness of God himself. Her drama traces the labyrinthine pathway the soul travels on its journey from loneliness to holiness. Impeded by the "powerful beat" of our culture which militates against a creative experience of loneliness, Sister Eileen felt only emptiness and senselessness. Whirling in circles, out of control, knowing only a repetitious rhythm, she asked her-

---

18. Lois Huffman, ed., *Whisperings: The Inspirational Writings of Tagore* (Kansas City, Mo.: Hallmark, 1973).

19. Bernard Bush, "Healing Grace," *The Way* (July, 1976): 189-98.

20. Eph. 3:16-17.

self why she was alive. In therapy, she was given the opportunity to creatively experience her loneliness, to confront and renew her life. As she worked through her psychological problems, God was present in the depths of her soul. Her loneliness was a prelude to a solitude of soul whereby she felt God's presence. She lived, felt, and was torn by the "no one" in order that there should be One whose Word would speak to her in the stillness of her solitude. By sharing her loneliness during therapy and during her performance yesterday and today, I too heard the Word and was renewed in my conviction that my purpose in life is to heal by affirming others so that they may experience the fullness of the Healer that is and ever shall be.

Reverend Joseph L. Hart, S.S.E., Ph.D., is a full-time psychotherapist at the House of Affirmation, Whitinsville, Massachusetts, and director of graduate studies for the House in conjunction with Anna Maria College, Paxton, Massachusetts. A priest of the Society of St. Edmund who was ordained in 1955, Father Hart studied theology at St. Edmund's Seminary. He received his doctorate at The Catholic University of America and did post-doctoral study at the Alfred Adler Institute in Chicago. Previously, he was psychological counselor and director of the counseling offices at St. Michael's College and at Trinity College in Vermont and instructor in the graduate counseling programs at St. Michael's College and the University of Vermont. He is a member of the American Society of Adlerian Psychology and has contributed to two of that society's journals. He most recently published an article in the October 1976 issue of *The Bulletin of the National Guild of Catholic Psychiatrists*. He is also a member of the American Psychological Association, the American Society of Group Psychotherapy and Psychodrama, and several other professional societies.

PERILS OF THE PLEASER

Joseph L. Hart

Loneliness is derived from just about anything in life: from our personal situations, from our culture, and from the institutions that society has created, including communities in the Church. Loneliness can also stem from our own behavior, even without our being aware of it, and it is this fact that I wish to discuss.

A few weeks ago on the Nova series, a television science program produced by the Public Broadcasting System, the film entitled *Benjamin* was shown. This British Broadcasting Company film was about an infant during the first six months of his life. There were scenes of his parents awaiting his arrival, graphic scenes of his birth, and some beautiful scenes of his first six months of life that showed how he communicated as an infant. The producers filmed such scenes by using slow motion videotape, sensitive timing devices, and various experiments including the use of an apparatus with an opening so the infant would see certain faces at different times. The producers recorded the infant's various responses. One could see this infant, right from the beginning of life, reaching out to people around him to communicate with them; and at times one could even feel that he was reaching out for a surcease of loneliness, that even at such an early age he experienced what the feeling was and sought means to alleviate it. The scenes depicted a social being, from the first moment of life to six months of age, interacting with other human beings in a very sophisticated way.

I remember some of the commentary. For example, commenting on the dialogue between Benjamin and his mother, the narrator pointed out how the infant was really "the more important person" and how he was "leading" his mother in that dialogue. Then the narrator mentioned how Benjamin was "controlling his surroundings" and how "he set up his father for play differently than he did his mother." One could see on film how he made such distinctions. At that early age he not only set his mother and father up for different kinds of play, but refused to play with a stranger until he deemed that stranger trustworthy.

LIFE STYLES: HABITUAL WAYS OF ACTING

Many psychologists have said that we form our reactions to others very early in life, and this research on the infant Benjamin supports that idea. Right from the beginning, we develop our own life style, a "script" so to speak, that is unique to us and that we carry with us through life. These scripts can be of many different kinds. For example, a person can "write" the script of a "controller," designed to either control life or be sure that life does not control him; or the script of a "martyr," designed to act the victim; or the script of one who is always right; or that of an excitement seeker or a pleaser. All these various life styles have a positive and a negative side. In other words, one's behavior can be on the "useful" or "useless" side regardless of the life style one has developed. The list on the opposite page contains a small sampling of possible life styles and their positive and negative aspects.

	Useful	Useless
The Controller	• good administrative ability • orderly, neat • an achiever	• manipulates others • dislikes surprises, spontaneity • frequently uses perfectionism to depreciate others
The One Who Is Always Right	• honest • respects right of others • dependable; his word is his bond	• puts being "right" above good human relations • inflexible; emphasizes "law and order" • might makes right
The Mischief-Maker	• likes fun; outgoing; an extrovert • adventuresome • risk taking	• despises routine; easily bored • quits task early; not dependable • commotion follows him like a cloud
The Pleaser	• a likeable person • easy to approach (at first) • appears non-threatening, non-judgmental • self-sacrificing; frequently a community "caretaker"	• "The person who needs to be liked feels required to please everyone all the time. Particularly sensitive to criticism, he feels crushed when he does not receive universal and constant approval. He trains himself to read other people carefully in order to discover what might please them and shifts from position to position in an attempt to please. He thinks of evaluations of others as the yardstick of his worth."*

*Arthur G. Nikelly, *Techniques for Behavior Change* (Springfield, Ill.,: Charles C. Thomas, 1971), p. 78.

I have chosen to concentrate on the life style of the pleaser because I believe so many religious and clergy have adopted this particular life style whose relationship to loneliness will become evident later. For some of us the life style of the pleaser is almost debilitating because it has reached such an extreme; for others it is within a tolerable range. On a scale of zero to ten, whereby ten is the debilitating extreme and zero is the total absence of the pleaser's life style, the behavior of most of us would fall somewhere in the middle.

How does one create the life style of the pleaser or any one of the other life styles listed above? We look again to Benjamin, who like ourselves when we were infants, was born into a seemingly erratic, chaotic world. How was he going to make order out of it? How was he going to "reply" so that he could control the responses of others and count on them to respond in consistent ways?

All of us were faced with this same task as infants and as children, and we each responded in our own unique way. We tried to bring stability to the chaos. The way each of us responded, the way each of us organized his or her responses around a specific goal, was the way each of our life styles was formed. If our goal was to please, we became "pleasers."

I am indebted to Robert Bartholow, associate dean, Alfred Adler Institute of Minnesota, whose research identified the traits listed on the opposite page as the "pleaser's cluster."* If in childhood, and by childhood I mean from infancy to about the age of nine or ten, we have developed many of the following traits, then we might want to consider if we have developed the pleaser's life style.

---

*Paper presented at the American Society of Adlerian Psychology Convention held in Chicago on May 26, 1974.

Now, and this is important, pleasers are *not* people who simply observe the pleasantries that are a part of our culture, who observe polite conventions, practice civility, etc. Nor are they religious persons who, for Christ, would go "the extra mile." Pleasers are persons who find their *significance,* their *value* as persons, in pleasing others; they do not feel significant unless they sense that they are pleasing others and that others like them. They fail to perceive their own dignity as individuals and strive to attain a mistaken dignity in a way that never can be satisfied.

The "Pleaser's Cluster"

Intelligent	• average to above compared with children own age
Good grades	• average to above (especially in penmanship and/or spelling, "conformity" subjects)
Hard worker, industrious	• average to above
Teacher's pet	
Helpful around home	• above average
Conformist to rules (school and/or home)	• average to above
Charming	• average to above
Affectionate	• average to above
Tries to please	• average to above
Critical of others (but quiet about it; may be a tattler)	• average to above
Sensitive; thin-skinned (feelings easily hurt)	• average to above
Idealistic	• average to above

High standards of right and wrong
Father's favorite (or wanted to be), or mother's favorite (if she was the more dominant)
Grandparent's (Grandparents') favorite
Had a sibling who was a rebel, a mischief-maker, or an excitement-seeker; therefore the "good one" by comparison

PROBLEMS OF THE PLEASER LIFE STYLE

I have identified seven problems inherent in the life style of the pleaser. They range from the *intra*personal, that is, problems pleasers have within themselves, to the *inter*personal, that is, the problems they have getting along with others. This is the sad paradox: pleasers constantly strive to please others; yet they so often end up alone, lonely. Admittedly, I find it hard to make these intrapersonal and interpersonal distinctions because all disturbed behavior is disturbing to others. In fact, a Chicago psychologist, Israel Golddiamond, has said that such is one of the purposes of disturbed behavior. I believe that practically every person who experiences intrapersonal disturbance simultaneously experiences interpersonal problems because this same disturbance disturbs others.

Let us examine first the intrapersonal and the interpersonal problems facing people with the pleaser life style, those who find significance in being liked by others and who cannot believe in their own value, dignity, and worth unless they are, or feel they are, so liked.

First, because their behavior is based on being accepted by others, pleasers suffer *guilt* feelings when they cannot please all of the people all of the time in every circumstance. Obviously, this guilt is not healthy because it does not lead to change. It is neurotic guilt (although real and painful), used to lessen a pleaser's feelings of inferiority when he or she fails to please another, to reach another's standard.

Second, pleasers practice *conformity* at the expense of self-determination. The pleaser attempts to conform to a set of standards that are not really his or hers, that have not been internalized and are external to the person. He or she tries to live up to these external norms and thus must shift positions for different people.

Father Tom Kane, executive director of the House of Affirmation, makes a point that I would like to repeat here. He speaks of how religious and clergy were conforming at the expense of self-determination in the old days. At that time, if one lived up to the Rule, one would find acceptance. Getting up when the bell rang and being in chapel at a specified time, for example, were rules that when followed would lead to acceptance. By no longer requiring these rules, the "new way" seems to offer greater self-determination. But, as Father Kane points out, pleasers still find acceptance by doing not what they themselves want but by doing what the group wants, what is fashionable at the moment. Essentially, the pleaser is involved in the same process now as in earlier days. He or she seeks to conform to something outside the self, to reach standards exterior to the person. Usually, the pleaser succeeds admirably in this goal. He or she readily meets other people's codes at the expense of his or her own self-determination, own value system, and own knowledge of what he or she stands for.

As we examine the pleaser's interpersonal problems, the loneliness element becomes more apparent. The person whose life style follows the script of the pleaser considers the evaluations of others the measuring stick of self worth. Thus pleasers encounter a third problem: regardless of who or what they are, regardless of what they do, *life is meaningless without someone's approval.* But, even when accepted, the approval a pleaser achieves is often short-lived. Because pleasers often doubt the approval others extend, they are constantly on the lookout for more signs of approval. Because the measuring stick of their worth is someone else's opinions or evaluations, they emphasize their *doing* instead of their *being*. This emphasis inhibits affirmation of persons.

Persons with the pleaser life style are usually hypersensitive, very thin-skinned, and easily hurt. Why, when the pleaser suffers internally, is such sensitivity an interpersonal problem associated with loneliness? Others tend to avoid the hypersensitive person, knowing that around this individual they must be very careful. Consequently, hypersensitive persons are often very lonely.

Depression is a fourth problem. Pleasers feel criticized even though criticism may not have been intended. Because pleasers interpret criticism (real or supposed) in this manner, they are greatly liable to feelings of depression. One criticism and their world collapses! Pleasers have expectations of how others *ought* to behave toward them, how others *should* behave toward them, and when the others do not behave such, depression follows. But this depression is really anger, unrecognized, but anger nevertheless, manifested because someone else has not lived up to what the pleaser expects of him or her. Pleasers, however, are too "nice" to express the anger or even to recognize it as such. Again the problem is interpersonal and again the consequence is loneliness. Either the pleasers themselves feel so miserable that they isolate themselves and withdraw, or others avoid them because their depression is so disturbing.

Fifth, pleasers *cannot accept compliments*. Counting overmuch on the opinions of others, they live a yo-yo existence; their worth is up and down according to those opinions. They find a compliment hard and sometimes even impossible to believe. "They are saying a complimentary thing about me to please me" is an unspoken thought that implies that what is said really is not true. The reaction is a variation of one of my favorite lines from Groucho Marx, who is supposed to have said: "I would never stoop so low as to join a country club that would have me as a member."

Sixth, pleasers *lose self-identity*. They are so tuned in to being liked by others, and to pleasing others so that they will be liked, that they lose sight of what or who they are. They may want to find their real selves because they have been living so much for and by others. When asked what they stand for, they may answer differently depending on who asks the question because pleasers will say one thing to one person or group and another to someone else, depending upon what they believe will be pleasing.

Seventh, pleasers *wear masks* to hide their inner feelings; so these inner feelings frequently do not match exterior appearances. I cannot help but think again of Sister Eileen's dramatic portrayal of this conflict. She spoke of masks and what a person feels inside compared to how he or she appears on the outside. The problem is that, in an effort to please, pleasers do not say "no" when they want to say "no"; they do not say "yes" when they want to say "yes"; and they find it very hard to say whatever they want. Smiling and pleasant on the exterior, they are angry and resentful inside because they are always giving and seldom receiving. This is one of the reasons why it is so hard for pleasers to achieve lasting and meaningful relationships with others. Their appearance is contradictory to their real feelings, and tension results. Deep and continuing relationships are difficult when superficial pleasantness masks angry feelings of being used.

Often pleasers think that other people feel the same way; so they refrain from making legitimate requests of others. Pleasers think other persons will not be able to refuse their requests; so, rather than impose on them and have them feel angry and resentful (as pleasers would), the request is not made in the first place. Thus the pleaser may have many unfulfilled needs that unfortunately and sadly result in feelings of loneliness.

Of all the perils pleasers face, one of the greatest is loneliness. Loneliness occurs because they cannot let themselves be real persons, be themselves, and cannot express their honest thoughts and feelings for fear of displeasing others. The body armor is too thick; it constricts. When others feel they are dealing with a facade (or a mask, as in Sr. Eileen's dramatization), they tend to distance themselves from the person, to avoid him or her. Again we encounter the sad paradox that the one who wants so much to please ends up lonely! Also, a pleaser is hard for a person who really needs help in a sustained way to approach because the parishioner, student, client, or whoever, soon discovers that the pleaser says what the pleaser thinks others want to hear, and not what they need to hear even if it might be displeasing.

Again the real problem is the script written early in life that results in pleasers' finding significance when they believe (or feel) that they are pleasing others and that others like them. This goal is so dominant in their life style that they really cannot be themselves.

ALLEVIATING LONELINESS

Loneliness is part of life; it is always with us. It has been with us since we were infants like Benjamin when we, too, tried to obtain a surcease of the unpleasant feeling during our first few months of life. It was with us when, as youngsters, we strove to meet the outside world —the first day of school, new playmates, breaking away from home, etc. We had this loneliness as adolescents as we struggled with mixed-up feelings that no one seemed to understand; and we felt very much alone and misunderstood in dealing with them. Loneliness is present throughout our adult lives—in sicknesses, in the loss of loved ones, in not reaching goals that we have set, in so many things we have to go through before taking the final trip—alone —that separates us from all earthly attachments.

Loneliness is always with us as a part of life; yet I hesitate to call it a friend. But I do not want to call it an enemy either, because it shows we are alive, that we have feelings; and it prompts us to reach out of ourselves in hopes of alleviating it. In fact, that is the positive side of this coin of loneliness: it helps us to develop social interest, interest in the affairs of mankind, to find companionship, to reach out to others from that loneliness in order to lessen it.

I, too, developed a pleaser's life style. When I was a youngster, I got good grades in school; I got along well with the teachers; I worked hard; I kept the rules at school and at home; I was a sensitive youngster. I was my one living grandparent's favorite. There were other aspects of the pleaser's cluster that helped me develop this life style, but none was so great as the fact that I had an older brother who was a rebel, a hell raiser all the way. As a youngster, I could really shine in comparison! So why have I chosen to discuss my own characteristic? Maybe I am borrowing a bit from the wisdom of Alcoholics Anonymous; surely "recovering" pleasers can best help other pleasers seeking to change their life styles.

After all, each of us is a pleaser to some degree. Pleasing is part of the human condition; facing this fact, being able to laugh at it, is half the battle. To know that we are pleasing, and why we are doing it, is in itself helpful. If we condemn ourselves for it, then we are really not accepting our humanity. Mistakes in our script, in our life style, will happen; if we put ourselves down, we are not being realistic. I think we have to laugh at ourselves, at least interiorly, to know that we make these kinds of mistakes.

Sometimes we religious look for perfection in religious life and try to achieve a moral perfection that is impossible to attain. We have to recognize that the ideal is quite different from the real and that spiritual perfection will come to us only after we are dead and buried a few days. To expect emotional perfection is also a mistake. An emotionally perfect person, psychologically "together," is an unattainable ideal. If we think we ought to be perfect, we will not recognize our mistakes; and hiding from one's emotional mistakes does not help. I am reminded of my favorite Irish expression: "When the ghost comes after you, if you run away from him, he'll chase you; but if you run toward him, he'll go away!"

If we accept as part of the human condition that we can be wrong, then we are free to take a stand and clearly express it, knowing that we have a right to our own ideas, opinions, and values as ours. They may be different from others; but we do not have to live for others, to please them, or to change merely because they *expect* us to or *wish* us to change. Only evidence should make us change. As Charles Schwab said: "A man who trims himself to suit everybody will soon whittle himself away." With regard to this whole problem of self-determination and of exercising our rights and desires, what we really need is *the courage to be imperfect!*

THE VALUE OF GOOD COMMUNICATIONS

The pleaser must learn to respect others enough to let them know what he or she is really and truly thinking and feeling. Such openness will alleviate the pleaser's loneliness as much as it can be alleviated in the human condition. The loneliness that stems from the pleaser's script is mitigated because communication as an equal and not as an inferior trying to achieve acceptance is more honest, more open, and more charitable. The pleaser I have described is not really charitable at all; he gives his neighbors what he thinks they want, and he does not give them himself. Good, honest, open, appropriate communication is charitable because when speaking thus we respect the others enough to let them know what we are truly feeling, and not what we think they would like to hear. We respect others enough to share with them what is really going on inside us, and that is charity.

I know change is easy to advocate but hard to effect, especially if we have been doing the contrary for years because of our early training and our life style. It *is* difficult to express our true feelings. We often think anger is most difficult to express, but many of us have equal difficulty expressing feelings of love. Love, appreciation, liking, compliments, and similar warm feelings and thoughts are not expressed in many of our religious houses and rectories because we fear to let true feelings, even these pleasant ones, be known. It is also difficult to state our own strengths and our own weaknesses; yet this kind of communication helps lessen loneliness because, when we do express them, we are out of ourselves and more deeply involved with another.

SUMMARY AND CONCLUSION

When we respect the right of others to know how we feel in response to what they said or did, then we are really being charitable with them; we are opening a pathway for communication that will diminish loneliness. Such communication also diminishes guilt feelings, fosters conformity to our own standards and values, and obviates comparisons because we then evaluate ourselves in the light of our own unique being. Hypersensitivity and depression diminish because we are involved in the give and take of human affairs; and *loneliness decreases as involvement increases*. It is then that we can accept compliments (and criticisms) and are open to receive this type of communication from others. The problem of self-identity diminishes because we are able to define "the real me" according to what we want and not what others want or expect (or are thought to want and expect). We become genuine persons who are seldom lonely because our contradictions between outer appearances and internal feelings are few. Masks are dropped, and we are then open to the real and lasting friendships that bring a lessening of loneliness.

Jesus was not a "pleaser"; that was not his life style. Note in the New Testament how communicative and assertive our Lord was. He in no way lived his life striving to be liked; he in no way lived his life trying to meet the expectations of others. When he felt weak, he prayed for the chalice to pass. When individuals tried to trick him into answering loaded questions, he was very assertive; he answered them when he wanted to and did not answer if he did not want to. He was a very open, communicative, and assertive person. I mention his character because so many of us religious and clergy who are pleasers and not appropriately assertive tend to justify ourselves by jumping on the "false charity" bandwagon; but we end up only more isolated, distanced, and lonely.

Reverend Bernard J. Bush, S.J., S.T.M., is director of the House of Affirmation, Montara, California. A member of the California Province of the Society of Jesus who was ordained in 1965, Father Bush studied theology at Regis College, Willowdale, Ontario. He served as student chaplain at the University of San Francisco before assuming the post of spiritual director at the Jesuit theologate in Berkeley, California. From there he went to Boston State Hospital where he interned in pastoral theology. In 1974, he joined the staff of the House of Affirmation and opened its Boston office. Father Bush has written numerous articles concerning spirituality and social justice, most notable in *The Way*. He has been active in the directed retreat movement and has lectured on Ignatian spirituality, religious life, mental health, and social justice.

THE FAMILY TIE THAT BINDS

Bernard J. Bush

I want to address myself to the problem of the enmeshment that sometimes occurs between religious or clergy and their families. I will explore some of the roots and causes of such enmeshment. Then I will discuss reasons why I believe such excessive involvement with family to be both dangerous to a religious vocation and an obstacle to spiritual, personal, and emotional growth. Since the enmeshment problem takes many forms, I will attempt to expose at least the rationalizations used to justify such involvement.

My conclusions are drawn from my clinical experience with a wide variety of religious persons. I have, moreover, had conversations about this subject with some religious superiors to determine whether they were observing patterns of enmeshment in their communities. They have assured me that, although enmeshment is indeed a problem, not much is being done or said to bring it out into the open. Thus they have encouraged me to discuss the problem more widely in an effort to generate some self-critical evaluation.

At this point I would like to inject a note of caution. The matter I am going to treat is highly emotional. Among the closest ties that exist in the human spectrum of relationships are those between children and parents, and between brothers and sisters. So what I am about to say concerning the need in some cases to loosen the bonds that tie families together can easily be interpreted as an attack on parenthood or family loyalties. That is not my intention. However, I am going to probe those relationships a bit, aware that there may be some sensitivity and defensiveness in reaction to what I am saying. Enmeshment is a controversial and nuanced subject which requires delicacy and good judgment.

I have no desire to advocate the attitudes of our contemporary secular society that treat the aged or infirm, widows, and the helpless as persons to be shunted off, ignored, despised, and kept out of sight as embarrassing reminders of our common destiny and mortality. I do not believe in cruelty, indifference, or neglect of parents. Thus, what I am about to say will not apply equally to everyone here. Some of it applies to all of us, and all of it to some of us.

The examples I will be using are composites taken from my clinical experience as well as from the lives of several of my personal friends. I am not revealing any individual's case history.

THE SCRIPTURAL THEME OF DETACHMENT

Essential to the vocation of any person who chooses to live a public and explicitly religious life is a sense of God's call to mission and one's personal response to it. There are abundant examples in Scripture of God's call and the variety of personal responses to the call. For example, in Genesis 12:1, God calls Abraham to go on a mission pilgrimage and to become the father of a great nation, saying, "Go forth from the land of your kinfolk and from your father's house to a land that I will show you." Abraham then left all behind, got up and went as he was told, and became the paradigm of every pilgrimage in faith since that time.

The teaching of Jesus, along with the example of his

relationship with his own family, particularly his mother, illustrates the same theme of detachment. When Mary and Joseph found Jesus in the temple, he said simply, "I must be about my Father's business" (Luke 2:49). He proclaimed at that early age his understanding of himself as a man on a mission. After the fashion of Abraham, this man was detaching himself from family ties in order to do what he felt he had to do in response to his Father's call. Later in his career, when he faced his own uncertainty about the timing of the call, it was his mother at the wedding feast who, in her own discerning way, opened the door for his entry into the period of his public ministry. When the woman from the crowd extolled Mary's motherhood in his regard by saying, "Blessed is the womb that bore you, and the breasts that nursed you," he replied, "Rather blessed are those who hear the word of God and keep it" (Luke 11:27-28). Jesus was proclaiming that his mother's greatness was in the fact that she had heard and responded to the word of God in her life and that that was what he was also doing. The time when his mother wanted to see him but was prevented by the crowd around him, he said, "Who is my mother, who are my brothers and sisters?" Then looking around at the group, he said that they were his mother and brothers and sisters when they followed the Father's will (Matthew 12:46-50). He declared that the imperatives of the ministry determined his loyalty and that those he was teaching and ministering to formed a familial bond with him. Jesus also discovered from his own unhappy experience in Nazareth, along with reflection on the prophets who went before him, that it was impossible to minister to people to whom he was bound by ties of personal familiarity.

These and many other texts, such as those that em-

phasize enmity between son and father for the sake of
the kingdom (Matthew 10:34-37) and those that emphasize radical detachment, "those who put their hand to
the plow" (Luke 9:52-62), have formed the scriptural
basis for many of the rules that prevented religious
from having extended contact with families. The precise
injunctions varied from community to community; but
I think it is generally true to say that involvement with
family was reduced to bare civility and sometimes not
even that was allowed. I think that for the most part
whatever wisdom is contained in such rules was largely
lost because friendships, which should have replaced familial ties for the continuation of the maturing process,
were strictly prohibited. A kind of impersonality was
characteristic of religious life. Yet there was a wisdom
in those rules and injunctions since they enforced a detachment from family that was a protection for the
religious. They made it possible for the religious to pursue
goals and a style of life without undue interference, or
any interference for that matter, from parents who
might otherwise have been tempted to be overprotective
of their children. However, the overprotective atmosphere
of the convent or seminary frequently allowed a gap to
grow between intellectual, spiritual, and physical growth,
which continued, and emotional and social growth, which
was arrested.

SETTING PROPER PRIORITIES AND LIMITS

By a kind of analogy, a religious can be considered one
who has married a community through perpetual affiliation by means of vows, promises of mutual fidelity, sharing of goods and talents, acceptance of common goals, and
so forth. If, then, the case arises wherein the family of

the religious interferes with the pledged relationship in any substantial way, there is, again by analogy, the ingredients of the classic in-law problem. Just as a married person can neglect spouse and family to attend to the needs and demands of parents or brothers and sisters, so, too, a religious can devote energy to family that should be channeled into community and apostolate. Now, obviously, there is need for balance and good judgment here. However, I do not want to underestimate or dilute the force of what I am asserting since I believe that enmeshment is a widespread and serious problem in the church today.

For example, I know priests who call their mothers every night and spend half an hour on the telephone telling their mothers what they had for dinner, who came to see them, what was said to whom, parish or community problems, and gossip. I am speaking of men in their forties, fifties, and even sixties. If for some reason the call is not made, there is much recrimination that the man is neglecting his poor old mother or father, is not a loyal son, or is even unchristian because he did not call. Who can dispute such logic? Are not the ties of blood thicker than any other? Is not a son or daughter obligated to a parent in ways that can be repaid only by including the parent in all the activities of his or her life? In our culture, wherein parents in their later years derive so much of their satisfaction through the successes of their children, it is simply unthinkable that religious, particularly, would deprive them of that joy.

These attachments often go to incredible extremes. Many religious and priests spend most of their free time at home. They plan their vacations so that they can travel with their parents or spend extended periods of time with them. There are often economic reasons for this involvement, when the enticement of the family paying for a vacation or trip, which would be otherwise impossible because of a limited budget, proves to be the decisive factor. However, there are often more subtle and deeper emotional needs that are being satisfied in the process.

Quite often the priest or sister is manipulated by a family conspiracy into feeling guilty for not caring for aging parents. The religious is the child who is presumably free and unencumbered by the burdens of a family of his or her own. Anyone can readily understand the reluctance of a married child to care for aging parents, or even the impossibility of his or her doing so, but, from the family's point of view, few people would understand such reluctance or impossibility on the part of a religious. After all, the religious has abundant free time, no outside responsibilities, and now no rules to prohibit such involvement.

Recently an angry parishioner told me her pastor was unavailable to help her because he was living at home with his mother who was dying of cancer. This situation prevailed for eight months. It seems that the mother adamantly refused to go to a perfectly adequate chronic care facility and wanted to die at home. Her married sons and daughters refused to tend her at home but said that they would be willing to visit her and care for her needs if she would go to the hospital. When she still insisted on staying at home, the family prevailed upon the priest son to move in with her until she died. It appeared to me, hearing the story, that there was a serious question of his neglecting his parish responsibilities by such a decision. Yet in some ways his action seems quite reasonable. My impression from this and similar situations is that married children set proper priorities and limits more often than religious do. Even the parishioner who was being neglected in the process felt shame at being indignant with the priest who was so manifestly doing what any dutiful son should be doing.

IS LONELINESS THE MOTIVATION?

My belief, based on observation and work with religious who become enmeshed with their families, is that loneliness is often one of the motivating factors. Now that religious community life and, to some extent, parish life, are not as highly structured as they once were, many are seeking secure and familiar surroundings and relationships wherein they feel needed, respected, and cared for. Families are preeminently qualified to provide for these needs. A mutual dependency with all the attendant expectations can quickly grow when there is loneliness on both sides. For religious or priests to develop friendships that are personally enriching requires skills for relating that were not part of their training. Closeness and mature intimacy with peers of one's choice are frightening realities for many who have spent most of their lives since adolescence relating in ways that were spelled out by rule or duty. Thus it is not surprising that reintegration into family often provides the line of least resistance and is the most risk-free way of satisfying social needs.

Yet solving the anguish of personal loneliness in this way is full of emotional, spiritual, and personal dangers. If the religious feels in any way guilty about spending an excessive amount of time and energy with the family, crises of various sorts can and often are created that provide handy excuses for the involvement. The religious is satisfied because he or she feels needed, and the parents are satisfied because now they know they will be taken care of. However, such mutual dependency very seldom contributes to maturity since the child is still being related to as just that, a child. It is as if the religious had never left home in the first place. It is rare in such circumstances that the enmeshed priest, brother, or sister actually feels like an adult at home. Very often when I question them about their feelings, they report that their mothers or fathers still treat them like a child and that they feel like a child. The case of one priest I am working with is not atypical. Whenever he stays overnight at home, his mother puts an 11:00 p.m. curfew on him. Moreover, she quizzes him about whom he was with, where he went, and what he did, and he dutifully reports all the details to her for her approval. He is fifty-three years old.

Many parents of religious sons or daughters are overprotective. In our religious culture, there is a certain pride taken by parents in the fact that their child is a religious or priest. This is not in itself bad. One of the important by-products of parenthood is to enjoy and be enriched by the accomplishments of one's children. The problem arises when the parents need their children to succeed and thus interfere in their lives in order to ensure that they do. The case of the overprotective mother cited above illustrates this point. She gets her own sense of importance out of the fact that her son is a priest. And she is doing everything she can to see that he lives up to her expectations of what a good priest should do so that he will be a credit to her. She is communicating to him that she still considers him to be under her motherly care and that it would be a great disappointment to her should he fail her in any way. He, for his part, fosters this dependency and cannot untie the apron strings for fear of hurting her. Yet this relationship, unhealthy as it is in so many ways, is rationalized as doing his duty to his parent. What most of us fail to understand is that parents have a remarkably high ability to survive in the face of adversity. They are not nearly as fragile as they sometimes present themselves or as perhaps we need them to be. I wonder who took care of parents before the home visiting rules of religious communities were changed. There is material for meditation here. Surely the God who clothes the lilies of the field has and will continue to provide for parents.

One of the causes of this problem from the side of the parents is that they have not developed interests outside of rearing their families. Mothers and fathers whose sole concern was to provide for their children, sometimes at the expense of growing in their relationship to each other, and who do not have interests, hobbies, friendships outside of their children, face a barren old age when the children are gone. Their plight has been called the "empty nest syndrome." When it occurs, and there is a corresponding loneliness on the side of the religious or priest, there develops an almost irresistible pull to get together to alleviate their mutual loneliness. The parent is then allowed to regress to a childish state of dependence. The responsibility of caring for such regressed parents engenders a sense of maturity; but it is a pseudo-maturity. The relationship is still parent-child, but with the roles reversed. The effect that the reversal has on the religious is to foster and encourage the same problem that the parents have. Much time and energy are used growing in dependency rather than in maturity.

GUILT DISGUISED AS CHARITY

A common rationalization for running home to parents at every opportunity is that "charity begins at home." I contend that it is not charity that most often motivates such enmeshed relationships, but guilt. I frequently hear the complaint, "I feel so guilty when I do not take care of them." The guilt is of course compounded when the religious is doing something for himself rather than going home. The thought of the poor parent at home alone and suffering makes the enjoyment of personal interests almost impossible. It is easy to see that when this situation exists, the stage is set for all kinds of demands and manipulations to be made. Parents can and often do create problems, preferably problems that have no solution, in order to keep their children close to them. This is not to say that the problems are not real. They are. Financial worries, alcoholism, depression, old age disability, and various infirmities are real enough. The illusion is that the priest or religious son or daughter has the time and resources to solve them. When there is a case of real need and deprivation, the entire community should become involved to help solve it, not just the individual who belongs to the family. And, by whole community, I mean city, state, religious, charitable, and other agencies that are set up precisely to help in such situations.

THE DANGER OF ENMESHMENT AND WHAT CONTRIBUTES TO ENMESHMENT

Although I have never before heard it identified this way, I would say that enmeshment with family is a form of "secular worldliness" that is dangerous to a religious vocation. It distracts and turns the religious away from his or her chosen goal and life style as surely as any other kind of completely absorbing secular involvement. Enmeshed family relationships are a closed world based only minimally, if at all, on religious values. They foster unhealthy dependencies, provide false security, and inhibit emotional growth. I believe that when these conditions exist, and they exist far more frequently than is generally admitted, there is a real danger to the vocation of the religious or priest who is thus involved.

It might be good here to point out some aspects of religious community and rectory life that contribute to the problem. It is obvious to all that profound changes are taking place in the structure of religious life in the Church. For one thing, communities are rapidly destructuring, leaving the individual sister, brother, or priest with more autonomy and responsibility to organize his or her life. There is more freedom to socialize with persons of one's own choice, to pray when and how one wishes, to develop interests and recreations based on one's own felt needs. Considerable personal strength and integrity are required to attend to such personal developmental needs as they arise. We religious simply do not have anyone in authority telling us when to get up, when to eat, when to pray, to whom to talk, where we can go, how, and with whom. These decisions must be made by the individual. For many, this responsibility is frightening because, never in the past allowed to make these decisions, they were not trained to accept such responsibility. For some, the experience of other sisters in an apartment going their separate ways, while they are left behind alone, engenders feelings of anxiety and fear. To follow the line of least resistance is to return to the home where one is loved, respected, cared for, and secure.

Some might object to my calling "going home to relieve

loneliness" the line of least resistance. They might say that, in fact, it is a terrible burden to go home. They will tell me the problems, tensions, verbal and nonverbal hostilities, and other unpleasant experiences they have at home. They might say that they would rather be with their many friends than with their family. However, when I ask them how they would feel if they went out with those friends and let their families solve their own problems, almost invariably they say they would feel guilty. Since relieving the guilty feeling is preferable to enduring it and working it through to its unreasonable roots, going home is indeed the line of least resistance. From a spiritual point of view, taking this line of least resistance can represent an attempt by the religious to escape the dereliction-anxiety experience of the cross which he or she has pledged to embrace.

I mentioned earlier that such practice is dangerous emotionally. By now, I think it is clear that this is so. Parents who are needy have a very hard time adjusting to the fact that their children are mature adults. This is especially true in the case of religious, because sisters, brothers, or priests do not have much in the way of tangible signs that they are adults, save a few grey hairs. For example, married sons and daughters generally have children of their own to prove their adulthood. They have made their parents into grandparents. But in the case of the religious, without this evidence of independent adult responsibility, parents slip into considering their grown-up religious child the way they did when he or she left home, usually as an adolescent. It is impossible for the religious, who may be in a crisis of adult identity anyway, to grow up emotionally in that environment. Adult self-consciousness is developed through peer relationships and friendships with the same and opposite sexes. Yet that is precisely what is most interfered with by the demands of overprotective parents of religious.

ENMESHMENT IMPEDES VOCATION

There is a kind of single-mindedness and single-heartedness that is required for the pursuit of the kingdom on the part of religious or priests. It is our profession. St. Paul alludes to the difficulty of serving a wife or husband and giving undivided attention to the kingdom in 1 Corinthians 7. Jesus speaks of it when he encounters the rich young man and goes on to preach detachment from mother, father, wife, children, and property (Matthew 19:16-30). Pursuit of the kingdom includes many ingredients. Much less now than previously are we striving for perfection in terms of living up to some external law or rule, or slavishly imitating the saints. We have recently assumed more responsibility for our human growth into the fullness of Christ. We must now attend to our spiritual growth in more personal ways. Likewise, we must now devote time and energy to growing to mature adulthood with all our feelings and sensitivities intact, flourishing, and under control. To achieve this emotional as well as intellectual and spiritual maturity in the world we face today is a task that will challenge each of us for a lifetime. There is no point of arrival at growth until our life is ended. In the context of personal growth continuing throughout life, going home to mother or father to alleviate distress represents a regression. It is very easy to construct a walled-in world with family at a time when the apostolic movement is calling us to share the consciousness of Christ with global concerns. Enmeshment with parents is self-protective at a time when our vocation more than ever calls us to risk in faith for service to those in need and for personal development. Our call is to leave behind the things of the past in order to discern what God is doing new (Isaiah 43:18-19). We are more likely to find things of the past in our families rather than in what God is doing new.

An example might illustrate what I have been saying. For some time now I have been working with a sister whose father is a severe alcoholic. She devotes much time and energy to worrying about him, responding to his calls for help, and even at times going to the local jail to bring him home. It has become an expected practice for the sister to call her father every night to determine that he is well. One week she tried on several occasions to phone him and there was no answer. Her anxiety grew as the days went by. Finally, on the fourth day, she reached him and told him that she had been worried and that she had been unable to reach him. His reply was that if she really cared about him, she should have driven to his home to look in on him. She felt ashamed, embarrassed, and enormously guilty that she had not done that. When I suggested that she had a choice of action and that she could, if she wanted, tell him that unless and until he joined Alcoholics Anonymous, stopped drinking, and got his life in order, she would not call him at all, she became quite indignant and accused me of advocating cruelty to her parent. Emotionally, this sister prefers to be miserable with her father than to assume the responsibility of developing her own life and interests. The latter is by far the more frightening prospect for her. Needless to say, as long as she remains enmeshed with her father, she will have almost no opportunity to grow emotionally and will give only half attention to community living, apostolate, and her spiritual life.

The situation with diocesan priests is slightly different from religious. Religious men and women were not allowed to go home or have much contact with family, especially during the formation years. Visits were restricted to a few hours a month. Diocesan seminarians generally returned home for summer vacations and other times. In fact, until recently it was part of the spirituality of diocesan clergy to devote a day a week to their family as part of their loyal duty. The Blessed Virgin Mary and their mothers were to be the only two women in their lives. Mothers understood this and took up the task of protecting the virtue of their seminarian and priest sons. Fortunately, the situation is vastly improved now; but the practice lingers on very strongly in some diocesan clergy. A mother never lost her son when he went into the priesthood, and she had a legitimate complaint if she did not hear from him frequently because part of his spirituality was a duty to stay in touch with her and visit once a week.

Before I close this presentation, I would like to refer to the cautions I expressed earlier. I am aware that much of what I have said can be taken as promoting a coldness or indifference to parents. That was not my desire. Love of parents is a gospel value and an important part of our self-identity. However, an adult does not owe his or her parents the filial obedience of a child. It is a disorder in the relationship when parents interfere with the chosen life style and commitments of their children. Thus it is the task of clergy and religious to set proper and definite limits on their involvement with their families. They must realize that enmeshment can occur in many and subtle ways once either they or their parents try to satisfy one another's emotional dependency needs. The relationship should be free, sensible, undemanding, and non-interfering. Each individual must face the loneliness inside and turn it into the means to develop responsibility, awareness of "inner space," development of peer relationships, and the contemplation of God in the world which is an indispensable condition for the full Christian life.

Richard J. Gilmartin is a full-time psychotherapist at the House of Affirmation, Whitinsville, Massachusetts, and an associate professor of counselor education at Worcester (Massachusetts) State College. He received his graduate education at Fordham University, New York University, and St. John's University. Previously, he was psychological counselor at Worcester State College; director of counseling and instructor in the Graduate School at Assumption College, Worcester; chairman of the psychology department at St. Francis College, Brooklyn, New York; and supervising psychologist at the Religious Consultation Center of the Diocese of Brooklyn.

LONELINESS AND NARCISSISM

Richard Gilmartin

I believe it was in elementary school that I learned the strategy of dealing with my anxiety about speaking before a group by volunteering to be first. Then I could relax for the remainder of the time that it took for all the others to give their talks. Since I am scheduled to be last today, I could not employ my strategy and thus now stand before you after having endured six hours of anxious waiting.

The significance of being the last speaker of the day also challenges me. I am reminded of the Biblical suggestion of saving the poorest wine until last so that the guests, having savored the better wine and having experienced its effects, would not recognize the poor quality of what was now being presented to them. But then the Christian twist to the event was that the best wine, albeit miraculously so, was ultimately presented. But then my anxious confusion does not get resolved when we note the high quality of what has been said here today.

Another concern about being last was that there would be nothing left to say. We speakers did not consult beforehand on what we were going to say. Each of us took the theme of loneliness and developed it along his or her own unique lines of thought. In essence, as a group we are twisting this human phenomenon of loneliness to expose and view different facets of it.

So far we have heard about the loneliness that comes from being a "pleaser," the family and its role in the production of loneliness, and a very personal expression of the experience of loneliness. My professional bias is that I view people from the psychoanalytic perspective; so you can guess that I am going to be talking about human needs and their relationship to loneliness.

It is easy to stand before you and define the problem of loneliness without having to solve it. But my goal in defining the problem is to give some intellectual structure to our existential encounter with loneliness; hopefully, some insight will result. Not that understanding or insight will solve a personal problem; it will not. But it can be the beginning of a solution. By using insight, we can begin to make ourselves into the kind of human beings we want to be.

Loneliness is something that I am sure each of us has experienced. In the existential sense, I can teach nothing new about loneliness. Nor can I provide a formula by which to get rid of it. There are no cookbook solutions to human problems because each of us is unique, especially in our unhappiness. As Tolstoy said about the family: "All happy families resemble each other, while every unhappy family is unhappy in its own fashion." The same could be said of happy healthy people. Hence, my purpose here today is not to tell any individual how to solve his or her own personal problem of loneliness, but rather to offer an intellectual framework within which we humans can understand our emotional experience of loneliness; such understanding, in turn, may help particular individuals come to some resolution of their own personal loneliness.

My topic is loneliness and narcissism. What I would like to do is to separate these two concepts, discuss them separately, and then, by pulling them together, determine if some characteristic of narcissism can help us understand loneliness.

LONELINESS

Loneliness may not be unique to humans; other animals may also experience it. I hope that I am not anthropomorphizing when I think any animal that experiences bereavement also experiences loneliness, since loneliness is a part of bereavement. Certainly, loneliness is not something that just clergy and religious experience; nor is it unique to any segment of the population. It is a problem common to all human beings, probably extending beyond humans to other levels of the animal kingdom.

We all know what it is to be lonely; we have all experienced this pain. It is something like depression, but different. It is something like anxiety, but different. Both depression and anxiety have elements of loneliness mixed in, but the experience of loneliness differs from the experience of depression or anxiety.

This loneliness is not synonymous with being alone, because we can be alone and not feel lonely. In fact, the absence of periods of solitude can lead to loneliness. Too much being with people, too much crowdedness in our lives, can make us feel lonely. A Poor Claire nun is quoted by Marcelle Bernstein in her recent book, *The Nuns,* as saying:

> Everyone who has dedicated his/her life to celibacy does suffer from a kind of loneliness. And it is possible to feel lonely in a community where you can't talk to someone. I feel less alone in my cell than when I'm with other people.

But celibacy and religious community are not the sole causes of loneliness. If non-celibacy were the answer to loneliness, then married people would never be lonely.

Neither companionship nor relocation will solve an individual's loneliness. Barrooms can be the loneliest places in the world, and cities such as San Francisco, although beautiful and exciting, offer no panacea. People are attracted to San Francisco not only because of its natural beauty, but because they believe that by being there they will find fulfillment for their lives, i.e., living there will make them happy. So many of the lonely from around the country gravitate to San Francisco. Statistically, it has the highest suicide rate of any city in the country. The lonely discover that moving did not solve the problem, and they now have no place else to escape to.

The loneliness to which I refer is not what philosophers mean when they speak of the essential aloneness of each of us as the angst of human existence. I think it is true that in the very depth of our being we are essentially alone. We are born alone, we die alone, and there is always a part of us that, no matter how intimate we become with another human being, remains essentially untouched by the other. Perhaps, as a prelude to faith, each of us must experience this angst. A faith commitment involves clutching that essential loneliness in the depth of one's being and, with it, reaching blindly to Being Itself.

Nor is the dictionary of much help, because it defines loneliness in terms of being "without companionship," or "solitary."

What then is loneliness? In my understanding of it, the word that comes closest to it is "alienation." Loneliness is what we experience subjectively when certain needs are deprived. As we subjectively experience hunger when our need for food is not met, or subjectively feel insecurity when we feel unimportant to, or disliked by, significant people in our lives, so, too, loneliness is the subjective feeling we experience when certain needs are frustrated.

The basic need whose frustration leads to loneliness is the need to maintain linkage with one's world. We experience loneliness when we lose that linkage or contact with our world. There are two basic aspects to maintaining this linkage.

The first of these is maintaining a global type of linkage which is what we refer to when we talk about finding meaning or purpose in our lives. We humans must find a purposeful meaning to our existence. We need to find something that helps us make sense out of our day-to-day existence. We need to feel, at least for ourselves, that in some way we are having an impact on another (or others), that our being alive is making some kind of difference. If we lack this sense of meaning, purpose, or impact, then we experience loneliness.

This is part of the problem of aging in our society, especially for those who find their meaning, purpose, or value in their employment. When they reach retirement age, they are told that they can no longer work. They then feel useless, non-productive, insignificant—and lonely.

A second aspect of this need for linkage or contentedness is on an individual rather than a global level. We humans need to be involved in a meaningful relationship with another person (or persons). If we are not involved in a loving relationship with another, we experience loneliness. There are many types of loving relationships, but their common denominator is reciprocity. The need to love is just as important as the need to be loved. One without the other is insufficient. To love without being loved involves pain; it is a non-affirming event. To be loved without loving is a burden, and it too can be a non-affirming experience. The need to give love is equally important as the need to be loved. Without this kind of loving relationship, anyone is going to experience loneliness.

Thus, what I hear when someone tells me that he is lonely is that he has lost his linkage with his world, either in a global sense of purpose, meaning, and value to his existence, or in the individual, personal sense of being without intimate relationships. ˙

NARCISSISM

Narcissism is a neglected concept in psychoanalytic theory. As a concept, it was first mentioned by Freud, and later developed by Eric Fromm; but it is conceptually still in its infancy. It was originally thought to be a sexual perversion, but now it is thought to play a more significant role in personality development.

The word "narcissism" comes from Greek mythology. Narcissus was the Greek youth who spurned the love of Echo and, looking into a pool of water, fell in love with the image of himself that was reflected there, and this image became the love object of his life. Thus, in the grossest sense of the term, narcissism refers to a loving of one's self.

The interconnectedness of loneliness and narcissism first occurred to me when reading Konrad Lorenz's book *On Aggression* (1966), in which he attempts to explain the nature of aggressive behavior in humans. Rather than defining aggression in purely reactive terms, Lorenz conceives of it in terms of a human hydrolysis. This hydraulic theory of human needs postulates: that there is a buildup of tension within the organism; that once the tension reaches a certain level, a release for the tension is sought; and that, once relieved, the tension starts to build again and the cycle is repeated. Analogous to what occurs in a piston driven engine, human physical needs, e.g., hunger and sexuality, may also operate on an hydraulic principle. If human aggression is an hydraulic need, then it is an innate human need that must be expressed from time to time, regardless of external stimulation.

I do not believe Lorenz has adequately explained aggressive behavior in humans, but his illustration of the hydraulic nature of aggression is striking. He describes an aunt who has periodic episodes of aggressive behavior:

> In the good old days when there was still a Hapsburg monarchy and there were still domestic servants, I used to observe the following, regularly predictable behavior in my widowed aunt. She never kept a maid longer than eight to ten months. She was always delighted with a new servant, praised her to the skies, and swore that she had at last found the right one. In the course of the next few months her judgment cooled, she found small faults, then bigger ones, and toward the end of the stated period, she discovered hateful qualities in the poor girl who was finally discharged without a reference after a violent quarrel. After this explosion the old lady was once more prepared to find a perfect angel in her next employee.

There is something familiar about this description. I am sure we have all either known others who have had, or experienced ourselves, good initial relationships that wore thin as time went on. The parties to such relationships first became irritated at each other and then distanced from each other. Such separation occurs frequently in marriages wherein two people, full of affection and love for each other, make their public commitment to a lifelong, loving relationship and, in a relatively short time, are not even able to talk meaningfully to each other.

Lorenz would interpret such distancing as a natural buildup of aggression; but I think there is another way of looking at it. Fromm (cf. *The Anatomy of Human Destructiveness,* 1975) interprets the same incident from a different perspective. Discussing Lorenz's aunt, Fromm describes her as a very narcissistic woman, one who looks for a servant who will be totally devoted, totally committed, with no interests in life other than meeting an employer's needs. The aunt hires a servant fully believing that this expectation will be realized. When her unrealizable expectation is frustrated, she reacts with rage and finds reasons to discharge the servant. Her behavior is narcissistic.

Narcissism has many forms. In its more extreme form, it is a state in which only I, my feelings, my needs, my properties are experienced as fully real, valuable, or significant, and everything that does not pertain to me is experienced as unimportant. Narcissism is the opposite of empathy.

Because narcissism has many degrees, it should not always be thought of pejoratively. Our goal should be to strike a balance between narcissism and empathy. Whenever we move to meet our own needs, we are, in the broadest sense, behaving narcissistically. When we move to meet our needs for dependence, nurturance, affection, esteem, significance, recognition, autonomy, etc., we are striving to satisfy our narcissistic needs; and, if any of these is frustrated, we experience a wound to our narcissism and react with anger. But because we tend to repress our narcissism, thereby failing to acknowledge our narcissistic strivings, we have difficulty pinpointing the hurt and anger we experience if we encounter frustration. So we begin looking for reasons to be angry, much as Lorenz's aunt did when she "discovered" her servants' "faults." It is obvious, however, that her anger actually resulted from her frustrated narcissism because the anger was all out of proportion to the irritation that one would expect to experience when adjusting to the "faults" of another. Marriage counselors encounter such disproportion when the reason two people cite for their problem is not commensurate with the amount of anger they feel.

The same disproportionate anger is often experienced when narcissism is displaced onto an organization, an institution, or a country. In fact, there is a certain amount of social sanction to gratifying narcissism in this way. We identify ourselves with an organization, an institution, or a country, and its welfare, its prestige, its success becomes our own. Thus many Americans felt extreme anger when their country's flag was desecrated during Vietnam peace demonstrations. These Americans were reacting to the wounding of displaced narcissism.

In marriage, one person frequently approaches the other with certain unconscious, infantile, narcissistic expectations which when frustrated will lead to anger. Thus the woman who approaches her husband seeking a father-daughter level of gratification, or the man who approaches his wife seeking a mother-son level of gratification, will experience intense frustration and anger. But, unable to acknowledge their narcissistic expectations for what they are, such men and women will seek other reasons to justify their anger.

Parallel situations exist in religious communities. When individual priests, brothers, or sisters approach others with unacknowledged narcissistic expectations, they often get frustrated and react with anger and distancing. As in marriages, their initial contacts are filled with good feelings about the other, accompanied by expectations of having found someone to whom they can really relate. Within a short time, however, they discover "reasons" why the person does not qualify as a true friend.

LONELINESS AS AN EXPRESSION
OF FRUSTRATED NARCISSISM

Freud makes a distinction between primary and secondary narcissism that we need not examine here. However, it is important for us to distinguish between pathological, or unhealthy, narcissism and normal, healthy narcissism. Pathological narcissism, which Lorenz's aunt exemplifies, generally cannot be resolved without the kind of professional intervention that is beyond the scope of this discussion. But normal narcissism, which we all experience, refers to the so-called selfish expectations that, if not satisfied, lead to hurt, depression, and withdrawal, thus setting the groundwork for loneliness.

How can we deal with these narcissistic needs? First, we must realize that we cannot eradicate them, for such action would be not only impossible but harmful to personality development. We have to achieve a balance between meeting our own needs and meeting the needs of others, between giving and receiving in interpersonal relatedness. If I only give, then I will surely experience narcissistic frustration. If I only receive, then others will sooner or later withdraw from me, certain of having been exploited. Good interpersonal relatedness requires a balance, for we are incapable of loving others without first loving ourselves.

Second, we must become aware of what is involved in our approaches to other people. We must become sensitive to our own needs and to the kinds of gratifications we seek in reaching out to others. Such sensitivity requires an openness in human relationships, i.e., a willingness to be ourselves, to let other people learn precisely who and what we are, and to listen to the responses of others to us. It is impossible to know ourselves without a willing-

ness to be ourselves. We cannot achieve real self-aware-
ness by sitting privately and engaging in self-contempla-
tion. We need others to objectify ourselves for ourselves;
the image of ourselves that we perceive mirrored back
from other people's reaction to us becomes how we perceive ourselves. Our self-concept is not formed from intro-
spection, but from introjection. However, in order to be
able to integrate as valid that perceived reaction, we must
be honest in the self that we present to others. If we act,
or mask, or in any way are phony in the self that we present, then we tend to reject the reaction of others to us.

Good relationships are difficult to establish, as many
married couples have discovered, because they require a
willingness to be open and honest. They are accompanied
by the risk of being brought face-to-face with those aspects of ourselves that we perceive as negative, or of admitting our own narcissism and thereby feeling vulnerable. They also involve the reciprocal task of verbalizing
our perceptions of others in ways that are helpful to these
others. In essence, then, to seek good relationships is to
risk rejection in order to meaningfully experience the
loving response of other persons.

Intimacy is the ultimate goal. In fact, almost every
piece of literature directed at religious professionals today
makes some mention of the need for intimacy in relationships, especially if the topic is celibacy or chastity. These
articles acknowledge the need for intimacy in order to
achieve personalism. But we must remember that this
need is not exclusive to religious; our whole society cries
out for intimacy, albeit many members are mistakenly
seeking ways of achieving instant intimacy.

Most clergy and religious are ill-prepared for intimacy.
Many of our families were poor models of intimacy, and

religious life before the mid-1960s discouraged intimacy and personalism. Religious were encouraged to become members of the order rather than persons, and intimate relationships were at least suspect, if not outrightly regarded as a violation of the religious commitment. Many religious even chose a celibate life style as a way of avoiding the demands of an intimate relationship. Now, practically overnight, expectations are reversed. Religious are expected to be persons, not merely members of an order; successful priests and religious are expected to form intimate relationships. But most of them know little about the dynamics of such relationships. They feel vaguely guilty because they cannot form them; yet they do not know how to begin. Unfortunately, no one has taken the time to prepare them, and there is no doubt that intimacy requires preparation.

I fear that a similar mistake may be made in relation to celibacy. Regardless of its value or lack thereof, optional celibacy requires preparation and can be considered only after the deeper psychological issues are resolved. If tomorrow celibacy were made optional, more problems would be created than would be solved.

Much of what I hear debated about this issue of optional celibacy leads me to the conclusion that the real issue is intimacy, not celibacy. Too often optional celibacy is presented as the solution to the problem of achieving intimacy; it is not. Genital sexuality does not guarantee intimacy. For proof, just look at the number of married couples who have a genital involvement, but who do not have an intimate relationship. Intimacy is much too complex to be achieved so simply. Genital sexuality can be a way of expressing intimacy, but it is certainly not the only way. Some of the most deeply intimate relationships I have known have not been genital.

What I do see as a step toward achieving intimacy is that openness and honesty that I spoke of earlier: an openness to ourselves and to others. More and more I see a need for small group experiences among religious and priests. Marriage encounter groups are proving extremely valuable to married couples; similarly, the group experience would help religious. Whether it be T-group, encounter group, sensitivity group, or what have you, the group can facilitate achieving insight into ourselves, discovering that our problems and needs are not unique, and learning openness, expressiveness, and responsiveness. I would like to see these groups be intercommunity and intersexed, involving both clergy and religious together. They would not be the solution to all problems, but they would be a great help toward achieving the intimacy that each of us needs if he or she is to avoid the killing pain of loneliness.

CONCLUSION

I have focused on a definition of loneliness and on one aspect of what prevents us from forming satisfying relationships, i.e., the narcissistic expectations that we bring to these relationships. Overcoming unhealthy narcissism involves a willingness to lower our defenses (in itself a crippling form of narcissism, i.e., unwillingness to appear bad, misunderstood, queer, etc., in someone else's eyes) and to try to express our unique humanness. For it is only someone's humanness that we can love. I may admire the scholar, envy the brave, stand in awe of the powerful, but I can love only the human. Is not this the message of the Christ figure?

I would like to see religious stop scapegoating. So many blame a lack of community or celibacy for their loneliness; I do not think they are being fair. Certainly we need community. Those who attended the symposium last year know how strongly I believe in community. Each member has a responsibility to create community and to work at maintaining it. Granted, in some cases, there may be factors beyond an individual's control that make the creation of community impossible. But even then, that individual must make decisions about his or her life style, decisions that will ensure that his or her own needs will be met. We never give up the responsibility for creating our own lives. We should never let the impossibility of creating community where we are destroy our chances of creating our own fulfillment.

The same can be said for celibacy. There may be value to having non-celibate priests and committed lay people, but the achievement of intimacy is not one of them. Intimacy is achieved without genital contact; perhaps even greater depths of intimacy can be achieved without it.

To me, the issue of conquering human loneliness is simple. We must maintain our linkage, the linkage between our own existence and larger realities, which gives life its meaning and purpose, and the personal linkage between us and other human beings whose presence in our lives enriches and sustains us.

HEALING GRACE

Bernard J. Bush

Since I undertook to write this article* on healing grace in the light of our experience at the House of Affirmation, I have been listening with particular care to the troubled religious men and women who come to us. What follows is my attempt to articulate some reflections on my experience of that mysterious, mutually shared process of healing which takes place in the context of faith and therapy that is our ministry. I will give a brief outline of the history and work of the House of Affirmation and then add some observations on professional Christian life and personal identity as it is evolving today. Particular attention will be paid to those aspects of contemporary religious living that present themselves through our clients as areas causing or intensifying psychological problems. It is not my intention, however, to deal extensively with various psychopathologies we treat, as this is an article on spirituality rather than a discussion of psychology as such. There is a danger of over-simplification when making comparisons drawn from clinical experience with disturbed persons to religious life as a whole. Yet the people who come to us are from so many places in the world and from so many different types of communities and congregations that I feel justified in making some limited generalizations.

We are living in an age of rapid transition in which

*Reprinted with permission from *The Way*, July 1976, pp. 189-98.

there is evidence of both decay and growth. We can find abundant reasons for despair and for hope. It is only by listening carefully with a discerning ear to all the evidence available that we will be able to understand what the Lord is saying to us. It is my belief that the people who are hurting and confused have at least as much to say about what is happening in the Church and world as those who are seemingly contented. There is often an incisive candour in a person who is suffering that cuts through to the sensitive heart of the matter.

Within the week prior to this writing, I have heard the following statements from sisters, priests, and brothers of various communities. (The quotations in this article from clients are printed with their permission.)

> Living in a ninety-eight percent female environment is so sterile. I yearn for, no I am so lonesome for, real life.

> My rectory is antiseptic. The formalities are observed, but day in and day out, I never meet — I don't know what I am saying, but it is so. O hell! it's dead there, and I'm dead too.

> I have such a gut aloneness, that I don't know what to do or where to turn.

> Somehow I just can't shake the fear. I'm afraid all the time.

> My superior is kind, and tries so hard, but I just can't stop being afraid of him, and, in fact, I'm afraid of anyone in authority.

> I don't find community a vital life-giving experience.

> I deep down don't have confidence in my sisters. I always feel like they are judging me.

> No matter what I do I feel guilty. Even if I please everyone else, I can't seem to please myself. I am a worthless failure.

> I am coming more and more to resent celibacy. I don't know what it means. Not that I want to get married, I don't — and I do so want to serve God and his people, but something is so deeply missing. There is this man who loves me. We haven't

done anything wrong, but I'm tempted to because it's only
when I am with him that I really *feel* like I am loved. My
sisters say they do, and I suppose they mean it, but it just
doesn't somehow feel real.

Statements such as these, which are quite typical and
taken at random, provide a source for reflection on religious life as it is actually being lived day to day. The
people who said these things to me are not the malcon-
tents or misfits. In each case they were said by religious
who are functioning and holding positions of responsibility. They are considered in some instances to be the
happiest and most stable members. What shows is not
always what is really going on. Religious are exceptionally
well trained to keep the cheerful front and to avoid looking at the realities. Communities often encourage such
pretence. Some clients say that they dare not reveal to
their communities what they are really thinking and
feeling, or even that they are coming to us for help.

The obvious reply to what I have said is that of course
we all have our moments of loneliness, sadness, depres-
sions, and doubts, but is that not just part of the life we
have chosen? Why dwell on that? Is there not enough
misery around? The reasons for hope and confidence, the
signs of the redeeming hand of God abound. It is easy
to point out the faults and failures. It takes greatness
of vision and faith to build up rather than to tear down.
Why must we be continually reminded of the depressing
side of religious life?

It is the unique ministry of the House of Affirmation to
the Church to ask these questions and to search out the
truth in order to heal and reconcile in an atmosphere of
renewal and love. Our community is an international
therapeutic treatment centre for emotionally troubled
religious and clergy. It began in 1970 as the consulting

Centre for Clergy and Religious for the diocese of Worcester, Massachusetts. The original out-patient service expanded in 1973 to include a residential treatment facility in Whitinsville, Massachusetts. Since then two additional satellite out-patient offices have been opened. In 1974, I opened an office in Boston, and Sister Malachy Joseph Lynch of the Selly Park Sisters opened one in Birmingham, England in 1975. This expansion was made in response to the ever-increasing demand for our services. Each move was sanctioned and welcomed by the local diocesan and religious superiors. However, the House of Affirmation is a non-profit organization, incorporated in the state of Massachusetts. Its relationship to the Church, while not official, is close and collaborative. It is entirely dependent for its material functioning on donations from interested foundations, concerned members of the laity and clergy, and from donations made by communities and dioceses whose members come to us.

The variety of programmes offered by the House of Affirmation includes individual and group therapy, communications and growth groups, career and candidate assessment, consultation to religious communities and workshops on psycho-theological issues, an internship leading to a master's degree in clinical psychology, and creative potential development courses.

The founders of the House of Affirmation are Sister Anna Polcino, s.c.m.m., m.d., and the Reverend Dr. Thomas A Kane, Ph.D. Sister Anna, formerly a missionary surgeon in West Pakistan and Bangladesh, is a practising psychiatrist. She is presently the psychiatric director of therapy. Fr. Kane is a priest psychologist of the Worcester diocese and is executive director of the House. Both have impressive academic, religious and human qualifications for this work.* Since its founding, the clinical staff has been increased as the need for expansion arose, until now it numbers twelve. This includes psychologists, psychiatrists, an art therapist, and a psychiatric nurse. There is additional part-time staff who provide the ancillary therapies which fill out the programme. We also have a dedicated staff of housekeepers, cooks, administrators and maintenance people. The staff is as widely varied as the Church itself, with diocesan and religious priests, brothers, sisters and lay persons, married, single and widowed, men and women of all ages and several cultures. Many schools of psychology are represented, as well as widely diversified educational backgrounds and interests.

The staff and residents together make a unique religious community within the Church. The atmosphere at the residential facility is familial and dignified in a beautiful eighty-year-old mansion and neighbouring buildings in the rolling hills of Massachusetts. There are twenty-five people in residence, which is the maximum capacity. Fr. Kane aptly describes it as a place for the treatment of the whole person in a wholly therapeutic environment.

The House of Affirmation is a total therapeutic milieu

---

*For fuller historical and biographical information and more detailed descriptions of different aspects of our work, I refer the reader to the published writings of our staff: Bush, B., S.J., (ed.) : *Coping: Issues of Emotional Living in an Age of Stress for Clergy and Religious* (Whitinsville, 1976) ; Jean, Sister Gabrielle L.: 'Affirmation: Healing in Community', in *Review for Religious*, vol. 34, n. 4, pp. 535-41 (1975) ; Kane, Rev. Dr. Thomas A.: 'The House of Affirmation', in *Brothers' Newsletter*, vol. 17, n. 2, pp. 18-27 (1975) ; Kane, Thomas A., Ph.D.: *Who Controls Me? A Psychotheological Reflection* (New York, 1974) ; Polcino, Sister Anna: 'Psychotheological Community', in *The Priest*, vol. 31, n. 9, pp. 19-23 (1975).

with one permanent community and one which changes. In order to ensure a healing atmosphere and a climate of loving co-operation, the staff devotes considerable attention to its own interpersonal relationships. Time is regularly scheduled for the staff to meet to discuss clinical issues, enjoy one another socially, share areas of expertise, pray, resolve the inevitable conflicts that arise, and supervise one another. Care is taken that each staff member stays in good health and gets proper recreation. Decisions that affect the life of the community are arrived at by discussion and consensus. Thus the atmosphere among the staff is one of openness and shared responsibility. It seems that this human dimension, carefully attended to, is at least as important as clinical expertise for the work of healing, since it serves as a model of healthy community living. We are generally happy, hopeful, caring men and women of deep faith and love for the Church.

Our treatment philosophy, as the name implies, is affirmation of the whole person. Affirmation is the positive response to the recognized goodness of the other. It is an experience of a kind of relationship that is creative of the person. The opposite of affirmation is denial, or non-recognition and non-response to the other. The effect of denial is psychic annihilation. Non-affirmed persons have generally experienced deprivation of affection in childhood, which is later reinforced by the impersonality and task-orientation of religious life. When personal worth is unrecognized and unacknowledged by others, the religious comes to believe that he or she has no value. The non-affirmed person can go through the motions of a productive life and even outwardly look happy, but much of the appearance is pretence. Inside there is anxiety, fear, insecurity, feelings of worthlessness, and depression. Efforts to boost oneself and reassurances from others do not seem to touch the deeper core where the unrest lies. Such feelings then produce behaviour which is self-defeating, such as attention-seeking, physical complaints, excessive business, hostility masked by a 'cheerful' facade, addictions, futile attempts to please others, conflict with peers and authorities, and compulsive sexual acting-out. Such behaviour serves only to increase loneliness and guilt-laden depression.

These problems are not cured by intensified spiritual practices or facile reassurances that one is 'o.k.', but by the genuine love of another which is felt and makes no demands. Such unqualified love creates a non-threatening environment where the person feels secure enough simply 'to be'. An atmosphere of consistent affirmation gives the necessary personal space and freedom to each person to develop his or her human identity as the base on which to build religious and community identities.

Every person is constituted by an almost infinite variety of identities. Each one partially answers the question, 'who am I?' These identities are arranged interiorly by each person in a constantly shifting hierarchy of relative importance. The identity which at any given time is the most personally important receives the greatest amount of attention and energy. There are, however, some identities which are of greater intrinsic value than others. For instance, my family and name are intrinsically more important for knowing who I am, than is the colour of my eyes. Both, however, are constitutive of my total identity. In the case of many religious, the relative value which is assigned to various identities is not in conformity with their real value. It is not uncommon to find religious professionals who find their most significant personal identity through membership in a particular congregation. This identity by affiliation is followed in order of importance by priest, sister, brother, function; then by Roman Catholic, Christian, nationality, man or woman, the least important identity being one's humanity. Thus the objectively least important ingredients of personal meaning become the most important to the individual and receive the most cultivation and attention. In fact, until recently, the most important and basic elements of personal identity, namely humanity and sexuality, were considered evils to be overcome. How can grace build on nature when one's humanity is deficient? It is much easier, but personally devastating in its effects, to define oneself in terms of a role than to rejoice in the goodness of being a living person. In other words, there are fairly accurate ways of measuring oneself and thus knowing when one is behaving like a 'good' religious of a particular congregation, or a 'good' sister or priest, because that is constantly being spelled out objectively in documents or group customs. It is much harder to know when one is being a 'good' human, or a 'good' man or woman. This problem of personal priority of identities becomes more acute when the various identities are seemingly in conflict. A man finds who he is as a man in relationship to his complement, a woman, and vice versa. However, when the atmosphere of seminary, convent or rectory is so restrictive that it prohibits or discourages normal relationships with the opposite sex, sexual identity must be developed in relation to the same sex. This exclusiveness often contributes to mutual reinforcement of the worst aspects of masculinity/femininity and impedes the process of maturing. Finally, when one's identity is defined in terms of observance of rules and structures, and those rules and structures are called into question or changed, the person who is unsure of his or her more basic identity experiences an acute emotional crisis. Some of the signs of such crisis are feelings of anxiety, bitterness, scepticism, defensiveness, selective rigidity and awkwardness in situations that call for human responses rather than pat dogmas.

Religious professionals have been uniquely trained to be models of the perfect life with ready solutions to the mysteries of this and the after life. But we who once thought we were already in the promised land are now finding ourselves once again wandering around in the Sinai desert. We simply do not have the roadmap. The familiar landmarks of devotion have disappeared. However, we do have the special perspective of faith, the indispensable and unique point of departure for reflection to be shared with our fellow pilgrims. We are partners in a dialogue with the world, immersed in its life and profoundly sharing its questions and doubts. For this task, the religious person should be first a sound human being, striving for maturity in the normal human way: that is, through the development of progressively deeper personal relationships and friendships. Faith assures that we can have confidence in the presence of the holy Spirit who permeates the process. Through contemplative reflection on personal experience enlightened by the scriptural revelation of God's ways with humans, the religious prophetically calls attention to that presence. This witness may not even involve much God-talk. It can simply be radiation of the inner joy and richness of one's life in the spirit.

The reality is sometimes quite different. One sister recently spoke to me of her disillusionment with her community and with much anguish told me: 'It all came to a head at our province assembly a few weeks ago. I looked around at several hundred sisters and all I saw were pale drawn faces and no joy. They were all so tired looking. I then took a long look at myself and saw that I was the same. I don't want to live this way any longer.'

To rediscover the life-springs within, a therapeutic community such as the House of Affirmation, and by extension, every religious community, should be a place where truth, reality and faith prevail. The grace of healing is present in the community as a whole and in the individuals of the community. The same grace is given to the one who is healing and to the one who is being healed. All are called upon both to be healed and to be healers of others, no matter how much one may be personally hurting. It is my conviction that the grace of healing is given precisely at the growing edge of the personality. A person is healed when most exposed and vulnerable, and likewise performs the most graceful healing when the sore places are reaching out tenderly to touch another. When façade relates to façade, or even when façade relates to suffering humanity, there is a pretence of loving and caring. The head may be present to the other, but the heart is not. The grace of healing is mediated through the humanity of each person in the community.

In our special healing community, the House of Affirmation, the principal responsibility for creating the atmosphere, developing programmes, etc., is with the staff. Each of us has come to this work through a personal odyssey of suffering, healing, change and growth. We are willing to share this weakness, and it is our greatest strength. We are constantly being reminded of our own frailty and limitations. Yet just as constantly, we discover the unfolding mystery of the action of God in our lives. This confidence in the strength and love of God gives us the willingness to risk feelings and responses of genuine love to the goodness of the other which is more important for healing than clinical skill alone. However, without the clinical expertise, we could easily lose our way in the problems that present themselves. Our task is to be both loving and professional.

We have found that in most religious, intellectual and even sometimes spiritual growth has outstripped emotional development. The characteristic defense-mechanism of religious is intellectualization, in which feared emotional responses are cut off from and repressed by the intellect. Eventually the person becomes unable to feel anything at all. In our therapeutic programme, the religious can discover and actualize creative potentialities through guided trial and error, and incorporate them into the whole process of growth. Thus, each individual comes to understand the uniqueness of his or her learning style and pace of growth. Nothing is forced or unnatural.

Another important dimension of our life together is the opportunity for men and women to live in the same community, and to learn to relate to one another as persons rather than as objects of fear or phantasy. This kind of living sometimes gives rise to reactions that are characteristic of delayed adolescence. When such feelings arise, they become the material for guided growth toward sexual maturity within the context of celibacy and its limits. We have found that celibacy as such is not the main problem of most who come to us. It is rather the lack of affirmation and affection which leads to problems in the area of sexuality. Only a small proportion of those who have come through our programme have left religious life.

We firmly believe that our therapy is a work of collaboration with the healing spirit of God in humanity. This work demands much reflection and contemplation of where and how God is present with his healing grace in each person. In this prayerful therapeutic process, the neurotic barriers to inner freedom in both the healer and healed are discovered, exposed and removed. Growth in freedom and the consequent acceptance of increased responsibility demand deep faith in the incarnation, that God is among us in human flesh. Our goal, then, is to help religious with emotional disorders to achieve a balanced and integrated personhood, wherein all feelings are joyfully accepted and guided by the graced and gentle light of reason and will. To achieve this goal, we have provided a milieu where the process of conversion from denial to affirmation can be experienced. Our clients are becoming healed and are returning to creative service in the Church. Our files contain many letters from former residents and non-residents, testifying to the permanency of the growth and changes that have occurred in their lives. The sad part is that frequently the communities and work situations have not changed. At the end of the course of treatment there is a renewed sense of the loving presence of God at deeper levels of the personality and an increased desire for prayer. It is not uncommon for a person to make a directed retreat prior to discharge with an affective responsiveness that was simply impossible before coming to us.

I would like, finally, to make some observations about preventive mental health in religious community life. There is still among us a strong strain of moralism and idealistic perfectionism which compounds depressive guilt feelings and compulsive self-destructive behaviour. We find that many of the neuroses we treat are aggravated by styles of spirituality and community life that encourage religious to be slavishly dependent, to intellectualize and mask the so-called negative feelings, and to try to be happy without giving and receiving genuine affection and warm love.

There is also a tendency to consume too much valuable energy with introspective community reorganization and constant revamping of structures. This inward-looking tendency stifles the apostolic spirit of reaching out to others in their need. Meetings upon meetings can have a very depressing effect on people. Moreover, religious particularly need to be reminded that they need to say 'no', and set limits on the demands that others make on their time and energy. The fine balance must be struck between helping others and being good to oneself. This means that religious professionals need to find outlets for creative recreation and hobbies, and to develop the ability to have fun and 'waste time' enjoyably in ways that are more enriching than spending endless hours watching television or gossiping. Leisure time should be allowed for the development of friendships with persons of one's own choice, whether of the same or the other sex. For healthy living, time should also be set aside for contemplative reflection on one's own emotional and spiritual life in order fully to enjoy being alive and feeling. Prayer is time spent with the Lord, fostering an affective relationship with him. In an atmosphere of loving trust, I can bring my other affective relationships to the Lord, so that they may develop under the guidance of his spirit without fear of reprisal or condemnation, since they also are God-given. A community goal should be to strive to discover and encourage every aspect of each other's total life situation that is truly life-giving and affirming. Each person should be able to feel himself/herself as both a healer and as needing to be healed by others. Honest and frank conversation without censuring or judging is needed. There must be freedom to confront and challenge lovingly, in order to prevent an irresponsible permissiveness.

Thus our communities can become affirming when the persons in them feel that they are secure to be themselves, to make mistakes, and to find gentle forgiveness and deeply caring support one for the other. Our Church professes and proclaims that its roots and corner stone is incarnate love. Yet, ironically, most of our religious patients come to us because there is a devastating lack of love in their lives.

In conclusion, I would like to state with gratitude that the work of the House of Affirmation has been abundantly blessed by God in the few years of its existence. While this might sound like excessive self-praise, this paper was shared with our residents in a lively discussion before the final copy was made. They offered many perceptive observations and suggested changes, mostly where I had understated what they are experiencing of our healing ministry. Church leaders have expressed their unanimous approval and support of our work. We have come upon many shoals which have nearly destroyed us. In each case we have been rescued by a presence that can only be called divine. Hence we rejoice and have great hope that our efforts will continue to be blessed, and that our service and experience will make a significant contribution to enhance the life of the whole Church.

All income derived from the sale of this book goes to no individual but is applied to providing care for priests and religious suffering from emotional unrest.

AFFIRMATION BOOKS is an important part of the ministry of the House of Affirmation, International Therapeutic Center for Clergy and Religious, founded by Sr. Anna Polcino, S.C.M.M., M.D.